PERSONAL STORYTELLING

DISCOVERING THE EXTRAORDINARY IN THE ORDINARY

Dear Kalen.

you are the keeper of dreams,
adventures and mystery. You
open minds and show the
possibilities and opportunities over
the challenges and limitations.

Sam Thiara and
Adam Cotterall

Sam Thiara (signature)

First published in 2014

Ignite the Dream Consulting
Email: story.share.community@gmail.com
Web: http://sam-thiara.com
Twitter: @Sam_Thiara

10 9 8 7 6 5 4 3 2

ISBN - 978-0-9937581-0-2

Printed and bound in Canada by Lulu.com

Dear Kalen,
    It's been great to have you join our team at Chaffey-Burke. You kind and gentle manner with students and adults is greatly appreciated. I hope our paths will cross again one day. Fiondly,
Sandhya K.

Let me tell you a story…and so the journey begins

ACKNOWLEDGEMENTS

Writing this book was like a putting a giant jigsaw puzzle together. It started out as a jumbled heap; slowly, the pieces started to make sense and come together to show itself. I now stand here, arms folded with a look of satisfaction, and stare at the completed image...my life in story.

I dedicate this book to everyone who has provided me inspiration throughout my life and helped me discover the extraordinary in the ordinary. You and I may have met at an event, you may hold a piece of my jigsaw puzzle, or you may have stumbled across my blog and have gotten to know me through my writing there. However our paths crossed, we are now connected, and I am thankful to have you with me on this journey.

While there are many people in my life, there are a few that have been a tremendous help on this book that I wish to thank.

Adam Cotterall, for helping me formulate this book based on an idea; he started the journey with me and contributed to this book. He did not participate for the accolades; he believed these stories had to be shared.

Connie Chang and Will Swanston, for being the first to help me realize I could write. By building my blog and website, they gave me the voice, confidence and mechanism to write.

Joanna Juy, for painstakingly editing this volume and polishing the content for overall clarity and Whitney Law on her creative skills to design the cover and back so that from initial glance it is an appealing book.

Julian Fok for the amazing rebrand of Sam and Ilia Bykov for the images in the book. Both are talented photographers.

Rick Antonson, an author and close friend was there to be a coach and cheer me along this mental and physical marathon.

To my parents who provided me the opportunity to be who I wanted to be. There were times I questioned my path but they were always there to support me.

To my lovely wife Sadhna and my two boys, I hope the stories captured in this book and my blog leave lasting memories of what I have accomplished in this life along with the laughter and enjoyment along the way.

READERS SAY

Once, over a dinner with Sam, I realized that I'd stopped talking and had listened for a while in awe of the unfolding stories, and I said, do you write? And he said, "I'm writing a book." It is that volume that the reader now, with great good fortune, is holding...

        Rick Antonson
        CEO and President, Tourism Vancouver

I was once told a profound truth: that the story is the basic unit of human understanding. However, I've continually been amazed at how few people are either willing or able to tell their own story. Too many people believe that their story is boring, stupid, or doesn't stack up to the stories of those around them. However, if the story is indeed the basic unit of human understanding, how will we ever be able to understand each other, or truly understand ourselves if we don't learn how to share our stories? That's why the work of Sam Thiara is so important: he doesn't just tell people how important it is to share their stories, he provides them with a roadmap on how to do so.

        Drew Dudley
        Nuance Leadership

From YouTube to newspapers to stone tablets, the rise and fall of various media formats is well-documented. And yet, one truism through the evolutions and revolutions of mass and interpersonal communication is the resilience and triumph of storytelling. Stories help people to engage, to understand, and to survive. They also inspire. To this end, Sam Thiara provides an insightful overview of this most powerful form of human communication -- and gives individuals a roadmap to telling powerful stories of their own.

        Derek Moscato
        Ph'd Candidate – Communications

Want to transcend your everyday existence and find true meaning into that which matters? If so, be prepared to learn, have fun, and be inspired as Sam weaves his lessons through a storyboard of captivating tales.

        Rick Pasin
        Founder , My Education Room

In a world where the person with the best story wins, Sam's insights and breakdown of the importance and process of storytelling is an essential read.

Terry Beech
Founder, Hire the World

Everything we do starts out as a thought. A positive mental attitude and curiosity help make our desires a reality. Sam leads by example and sees the extraordinary in life. This book is a window into Sam's world, a fun and thought provoking read.

Volodya Gusak
Director of Finance, Solterra Development Corp

The title 'Coach' or 'Mentor' does not sum Sam Thiara up. The thing about Sam is that he never ceases to be a champion and an enabler of others. Sam is always in your corner, in the best way possible. This type of support is so profoundly rare in a world full of cynics and suspicion. I can literally think of thousands of people's lives—myself included—who have been overwhelmingly impacted by Sam's humanity and boundlessness.

Madelaine Simpkin
Student, Simon Fraser University

While most look for people to follow in life, Sam is different. Through his stories and sharing life experiences, he does not want you to follow him but rather walk alongside him. And such qualities make him Sam, his stories make him unique and he is a compelling storyteller.

Muhammad Sheheryar Alam (Shery)
Student, Simon Fraser University

Sam's stories and guidance has been the light at the end of my (sometimes) dark tunnel. He has always inspired me to reinvent my perspective and believe in myself. Sam has a natural ability to find the extraordinary in the ordinary. Valuable life lessons learned from his stories have given me strength to take many big steps in my life confidently.

Ravneet Dhaliwal
Student and Co-Founder, Math4me Learning Inc

TABLE OF CONTENTS

Here~2~There

It took great time, to write this book,
Please turn the pages, and have a look,
A poet I am not, a writer perhaps,
The words I wrote, are within your grasp,
I wrote for me, I wrote for you,
From a dream emerged, something to do.

Scattered about, my stories were a struggle,
Laying all about, like a giant jigsaw puzzle,
Pulled from here, added to there,
My life is before you, presented with care,
Many have helped, to make this true,
I appreciated all, who became the crew.

Within us all, there are stories to be told,
Times in our life, we are not feeling bold,
We say to our self, who would care what I say,
My ramblings and thoughts, within my day
It is the world who needs, to know you were here,
To not share with others, becomes my fear.

Within you is greatness, that I can see,
Anything you want, take the time to be,
I am here for you, every step of the way,
Time is precious, and while I plan to stay,
I want you to know, just how much I care,
You are just one, and I find you quite rare.

~ Sam Thiara ~

~~~~~~~~~~~~~~~~~~~~~~~~~

Introduction

"Everyone's life is an autobiography…make yours worth reading."
~Sam Thiara

For years I have had stories swim around in my head, floating without an anchor to hold them in place. These stories were personal reflections and situations that I encountered during my life. Every day occurrences held life lessons embedded within them. Like a giant jigsaw puzzle, the pieces seemed to be connected but did not make sense.

I started to capture bits and pieces; attempting to assemble some order, trying to make sense of them. I felt like I had something to share with the world but who would be interested in the reflections of an average person?

The first step in my journey was sharing my personal stories in an online blog. My blog was a forum to document a yearlong adventure called 'Sam's 50/50-2012' (http://sams50-50.com/), where I wrote about seeing the extra-ordinary out of the ordinary and capturing the most amazing things in 2012 to commemorate my fiftieth birthday. It was an amazing project and one that I recommend one should consider for a milestone in their life.

The personal stories collected allowed me to share my thoughts and pulled together many of the ideas for this book. One notable milestone in 2011 that enabled me to envision this book and to blog, was my TEDxSFU talk titled 'Discovering the Extraordinary in the Ordinary'. This talk focused on how individuals have the capacity to capture stories and to share them.

As people read my blog and heard my stories, they had a glimpse into my personal storytelling and began to find comfort and purpose and meaning towards their own life. Blogging helped me create a personal style and sharpened my writing skills. I discovered that similar to my spoken voice, my written voice was conversational, like speaking to someone over a steaming hot cup of tea. The more I shared, the more people would say that it was helpful to them.

Through this book, I would like to continue sharing my learnings and helping others. My hope is to enable others to discover their passion or direction through self-reflection; how small day to day things can be significant in a broader context.

If I was to describe this book and my writing as a visual, it would be two individuals facing one another in the centre of a room. One is speaking while the other is listening. A large audience surrounds them, trying to listen in. Those closest to them sit comfortably, listening intently at the discussion. Those farther away, lean forward, trying to hear the conversation and eventually leave so that others can take their place. Both individuals in the middle of the circle are me.

I am the one telling the story and also the one listening to the words intently; using my own storytelling to self-mentor. Those around me are bystanders who find comfort and relevance in the conversation.

This book is a product of this self-direction and reflection. I have mentored hundreds of individuals and engaged thousands, but I have never really had a formal mentor myself. Instead, I look within for the direction that drives me towards my goals.

I am also a person with strong conviction. Upon discovering a passion for storytelling, I found a foundation to write from and needed to do so.

This book encourages the creation of stories that will allow you to reflect and share. Write stories for yourself and you will find an appreciative audience. A story does not have to be memorized, it is your experience and you are the best person to tell it. This book can help you put your thoughts and ideas together so that you can realize the value of what you bring forward. We need to take that quiet story voice and create a mechanism for us to share. Do not let others dictate if your story is interesting or not, if something is important to you, it is worth sharing.

This volume also provides insight on what has helped me become an engaged storyteller and an accomplished speaker. Some of you may accept the content, exercises and dedicate the time; embracing the sentiments that are provided. Others may gloss over the content and perhaps take away a few key elements. Some may want to only read the stories for interest and appreciation. No matter your purpose, keep in mind I have outlined steps that have helped me write and tell stories effectively.

This is a new adventure for me but I firmly believe that the stories shared can help others or complement the journey someone is already on. I have written this book in the way we would sit, talk, and become immersed in conversation. You will find my thoughts to be authentic and genuine. I am sharing my life lesson with you; look within yourself and discover what you can do and embark on your own personal journey.

This book is arranged into four parts to help guide you through a process.

- Part One describes what storytelling is, why tell stories and what makes up stories.

- Part Two are my own stories and how applying a certain principle can help you understand your own perspective on storytelling.

- Part Three is your opportunity to build and share your stories.

- Part Four is a collection of scenarios with a question at the end of each so you may reflect and practice your own writing and storytelling.

If you wish to embrace storytelling and would like to build your own cache of experiences but may not know where to begin, I encourage you to work through the book from cover to cover and try the various activities. If you are a reflective person by nature and purchased this book because you wanted to read stories, then I recommend you review the contents of the book but concentrate on the adventures described in Parts Two and Four.

You will also notice *'Action'* items listed throughout the book. When you see the word *'action'*, it means that there is a practical activity to help work the mind towards storytelling. Activities are not mandatory; you may flag it for later or decide to stop and try it at that moment. As you progress through the book, you might return to previous responses and activities as your thoughts develop. The end of each chapter and back of the book also has a handy notes section for you to reflect, journal and write down your thoughts. Use this book and the notes to help build your foundations towards story development and sharing.

My hope is that you take something away from the book. Whether it has helped your personal development or because it has put a smile on your face, it has met my objective and I am glad I could assist.

By picking up a copy of this book, you will learn more about me and I would also like to learn more about you. Like a piece of a jigsaw puzzle, you are part of my life puzzle.

There is a little fear in me by sharing this book and my stories because of what people might think; however, the bigger fear is if I don't put my thoughts down and get the book out."

~*Sam Thiara*

PART ONE

It takes a thousand voices to tell a single story.
~ Native American saying

What's in a Story?

What's the last story you heard? What's the last story you told? What's the last story you lived?

Stories are as old as we are as a species. From visual stories such as cave drawings and Inukshuk stone formations used by those on long journeys to written stories such as religious teachings that are shared with the masses, they are often our most impactful form of communicating with one another.

Since ancient times when stories were shared around campfires and village gatherings, stories have been the mechanism to pass along thoughts, ideas and superstitions to others. Stories have explained the world to an audience without social media, phone or internet. Even to this day, there are many oral societies that still have stories embedded into their existence. Stories can be a myth that explains the lack of rain for the harvest, a fable to warn children about dangerous behaviours, or documented precedence setting examples to settle injustices during the time of a roaming judicial system.

From a personal perspective, whether we want to make someone feel happy, change someone's opinion, or inspire them to action, storytelling has shaped us from cradle to adulthood. Stories have been told, shown and experienced by us on a daily basis throughout our lives.

We "get" stories. Stories stick with us. Why is this? From a psychological perspective, human beings are fundamentally "meaning making machines" and stories are a powerful way to make meaning from our experiences and to convey meaning to others. You can see how important for a pre-historic human to learn from shared stories. Is that rustling in the bushes a sabre tooth tiger that will eat me or a bird that I will eat for dinner? We have learned and developed over time. Over hundreds of thousands of years, our brains have evolved to interpret all the various inputs our senses are constantly being bombarded with to create a meaning. Storytelling engages our senses.

As a result, the storyteller emerged as a position of significance. People would gather around to hear the elder, chief, shaman, priest as they shared their wisdom through story. It explained the way of the world and justified action. It was used as a mechanism to educate and solidify a cultural base and at times, the stories developed further to be entrenched into a religious foundation.

A basic understanding – you at the centre

What is a central theme when it comes to personal storytelling? While we might have other people's stories to share, the ones that we need to build are our own. It is about drawing on our raw experiences and transforming them into stories worth sharing. Understand that you are the foundation of the stories you build. We are the actors in our own stories and many times we are the central figure so we have to get comfortable with ourselves before we can really examine and understand our stories. A good perspective to start from is: 'What defines you?' This is a helpful point of reference to consider understanding 'you'. If you were to build your foundation, what words would describe you to others? There is an exercise later on that will help you better define and understand 'you' but at this point; it is worth trying to understand your own personal foundation.

I firmly believe that the saying *"Everyone's life is an autobiography...but you need to make yours worth reading."* describes how a combination of one's experiences creates one's autobiography. One's personal stories leave a lasting impression on those people who become a part of the story. Whether we like it or not, we are all creating and building stories. How do we capture our thoughts so they become part of our lives? Building an autobiography is also a reminder to continue challenging ourselves and build on our experiences.

When examining our own lives, we have a past, a present, and a future. It is by intentionally choosing, in the present (and understanding the past), we have the opportunity to create our future. This is not about walking forward while looking in a rearview mirror. The past reinforces where we have come from and is vital in building our foundation as a storyteller as we move forward. If we were to look at our lives as a puzzle, we do not randomly place pieces together in an ad-hoc fashion. There is some strategy involved to find familiarity with pieces and see how they fit together.

When we look at what makes a story complete, we see there are actors, a setting, and some journey they must travel. The story seems more vivid, once we add descriptions of colour, clothing, temperature, sounds, and smells. A story does not need to be the ultimate epic journey. If we are the actors, setting and the journey, our stories can reflect the extraordinary in the ordinary; we just need to build it and recognize its significance. If it is important to you, then it is memorable and has the significance to be shared. We live in the ordinary but embedded in the ordinary are tremendously extraordinary experiences. For example, I have been able to find purpose in simplicity through the distribution of jigsaw puzzle pieces.

I believe one of the cornerstones of storytelling is to be reflective and it is by being reflective that we can add purpose and meaning to our stories. I have developed a concept from the term carpe diem – which means seize the day. In my case, CARPE stands for the process I go through to discover and tell stories and this will be discussed in a later section.

CARPE, as you will see, is about discovering the extraordinary in the ordinary. I have been able to take seemingly simple things, ideas and concepts and transformed them into stories.

An example of the extraordinary in the ordinary

This story shows how I took a simple set of footprints in the sand and how it became an important workshop on personal and professional development.

I was in Tofino on Vancouver Island, British Columbia, and was walking along the beach in the early morning and I found a single set of footprints in the sand. This intrigued me to the extent that I sat down on the sand and studied them in great detail for a long time.

Who do they belong to? Why are these footprints here? What is this person's story? What are their trials and tribulations, joys and sorrows? Along with these questions, I realized these footprints would be gone the next day. A personal development workshop was inspired that day with four elements that helps one build an autobiography worth reading.

The workshop was not clear at first. Only after further reflection about the footprints disappearing that a personal development workshop called 'How to leave a lasting impression and not just a footprint' came to mind.

There are four main themes that help an individual author an autobiography worth reading, based on one's vision, choices, limitations, and persistence.

- **Vision -** *People have the ability of seeing with their eyes, but not vision the future.*

  When I was in a corporation performing my day to day work, I felt the need to change my area of focus and I chose road safety. Although I did not have prior experience in road safety, instead of giving up on this vision, I reached out to the road safety professional to learn more about the field. I had a vision of getting into road safety and I was going to do anything and everything to learn about it so I could get into the field. The journey took a year and a half before I was successful, but in the end I achieved my vision. How is that possible? Well, one must embrace a vision of where they would like to go and put all effort towards it. I was able to find the right champions and enablers to help me and never lost sight of my vision towards road safety.

- **Choices-** *Life provides choices—if you don't make the decisions, people will decide for you.*

  Years ago, I was faced with a life altering decision. After six and half years in road safety, my employer was offering contract buyouts to all employees. Although I enjoyed my role, I was feeling a need to move on and try something new – a transition. Everyone around me advised against it; not one person supported me in my move, instead I had much opposition. They said I was crazy to leave a stable position that I enjoyed. I made the decision and took the contract buyout, leaving a position and organization I was proud to be a part of. Two months later, I landed a position that brought the 2010 Olympic Games to Canada.

I did not let others sway me in my vision and I made a choice. My decision was based on uncertainty; if I stayed, the company controlled the degree of uncertainty, by leaving, I controlled my uncertainty. I needed to control my uncertainty so I made a decision that worked out well. I took a risk and it paid off as I got to work on one of the most amazing teams ever.

- **Limitations**- *We set limitations by our words of can't, won't, shouldn't and will not. We set the bar.*

  Limit the what-if's in life. These are realizations of what we could have been or done, and the regrets one has for not pursing their vision. One of my favorite TED talks was by Phil Hansen called 'Embrace the Shake'. Phil was an amazing artist who was afflicted by a condition that limited his ability to continue creating intricate art. Rather than giving up, he accepted his limitations and made it limitless in his art. We should not dwell on what we cannot do, but instead focus on what we can do. If we cannot get over, under, or behind that obstacle, we should realize when to ask for help. Look for the possibilities and opportunities instead of the limitations and challenges ahead.

- **Persistence**- *Do not let others prevent you from accomplishing your goals. You can attain anything you want.*

  Realistic expectations should be set. As much as we persevere, we should also be willing to take alternative routes, stepping stones, or detours to arrive at our preferred destination. An example of persistence in this case would be this very book.

  On multiple occasions, I could have given up on this book, shelved it or deferred it to the future; but my persistence has motivated me to keep going. The idea of completing this project and having a medium to share my learnings has kept me on task. There are plenty of opportunities but it is up to us to recognize them. If there is something you want to do, you are on a crash course to accomplish this. It might not be today, tomorrow or a couple of years from now, but if you want something, the only person to stop you from accomplishing your goal is you. You create your own obstacles and limitations.

All of these thoughts, ideas and stories emerged from a simple set of footprints; seeing the extraordinary out of the ordinary. This workshop is full of stories. They are my twists and turns in life. The realizations that I have had for what one can accomplish if your mind is set for it. If I did not come across the footprints on the beach, would I still have a workshop? Perhaps, but I travel through life looking at the world around me, like Sherlock Holmes does with a magnifying glass. If I can find all this meaning from a simple set of footprints, what are you missing?

The Foundation

To start understanding stories, there needs to be an established base, a foundation that allows some insight but not rules. Stories are organic, just like your life, and by creating rules, they become limiting. I am providing the following five points as to describe some basic aspects of story building and telling.

5 Points for Crafting a Good Story

Much like a book, essay or movie, your personal story has to have purpose and meaning; otherwise it might not have the impact or generate the interest in your audience. Ultimately, there are five key elements you should strive for and they are:

- **Turn an incident into an experience**
- **Make sure it relates to the topic at hand**
- **Your story needs flow**
- **Apply and appeal to the senses of people**
- **Remember your audience**

1)   Turn an incident into an experience
We can categorize things that happen to us throughout our life as incidents; never thinking about them in greater depth. Incidents are separate and not connected, or so we think.

Most stories have a root and sometimes they start out as a small incident. It is only by reflecting and thinking about it does it evolve into an experience/story. The key word here is 'evolve'. In order to possess significance, an incident needs to evolve and grow into a story with meaning. Be aware of the small incidents in your life and try to appreciate them at a deeper level as they can become trigger points for deeper memories. Later in the book we will talk in depth of turning the ordinary into the extraordinary but it is worth noting that a good story started from something small. Not all incidents will become a story and not all experiences are based on a single incident. We just need to be aware that we are writing, telling and living in a story.

Note that incidents can happen to us directly or happen to others but we need to reflect and think about them deeper. If something happened to a friend of yours, what does it mean to you? Can you take it and build around it based on your own perspectives? Of course you can. You can interpret an incident that happened to someone else through your own lens. Remember to interpret an incident into a thought out experience because that becomes the key ingredient of your personal story.

2) Make sure it relates to the topic at hand

You need to have a reason to tell your story or a desired response from your audience. Like a comedian whose favorite anecdotes can fall flat, as a storyteller, you need to have the right situation, timing and content that apply to the listener. The story has to be relevant to current situation.

One way that this can work is to actively listen and observe. Understand what is being discussed so that you can collect your thoughts and observe the people in the conversation. It is not about trying to squeeze your story into every setting but rather looking for the cues for the best time to express it.

It is important to take the time to prepare and understand your audience but not in a mechanical and systematic way. Try to build and share stories that are aligned with the listener's needs and wants. You may be unsure of what their expectations are, but if you take the time to listen to the audience, you will build that understanding. By understanding the listener and their reason for listening to you, then you obtain the foundation to align your story towards for a desired impact.

For example, if I am speaking to university students on their own personal and professional development, they are not there to hear me tell jokes. They want meaningful stories and I make sure to select stories that are relevant to their objectives. By sharing my stories, they/we have connectedness and shared associations.

As you compile your stories and make them into experiences, build a collection of stories (on a mental bookshelf) and be aware of which stories can be applied to which audiences and situations for greatest appreciation.

People might think that storytelling is about just that, 'telling' but it is more than that. Storytelling is about the application and appropriateness. Do not discount your listener, in many instances I have look to them for the cues on what stories I should share.

3) Your story needs flow

As you think about a story you heard or a movie you watched, what is it about the piece that appealed to you? Think about the storyteller or what you have seen and you likely will find that it flowed.

The art of storytelling is about creating a flow of incidents and imagery that creates understanding. You need to set the scene and use descriptors to walk the audience through your images and then try to relay a purpose, moral or lesson. Remember, the listener can relate to your story but they may not have had the same experience as you have. To have impact, it helps to have something climactic. A climactic aspect does not need to be epic or life changing; it can simply be identifying the extraordinary in the ordinary. The climactic piece anchors your story.

The idea is to build up the story so the key point/element rises to the surface and becomes the reason to tell the story. By incorporating purpose, morals or lessons, the story teller relays something to the listener. This does not have to be in every instance but compelling stories often have purpose and meaning. When I tell my stories, some of them are for an audience that wants to hear something simple and interesting while others are looking for significance.

Try to think of your story as writing an essay; it needs to have an introduction, body and conclusion. Without a strong introduction, it is unclear why the story is being told. An interesting introduction can help capture the imagination of your listener. The body provides the descriptors, images and details of our story, the conclusion is restating the reason you told the story. Each part is important for the accomplished storyteller because without the introduction, it is like walking into a movie theatre midway through the movie. Without the conclusion, your story just ends without purpose. Without a strong body, the audience misses key components that support the reason for the story.

Introduction:

Your introduction should start strong and relate to the topic in hand. It should capture the attention of the listener/reader right at the outset so they want to continue to read your story. You will need to be creative in how you do your start. Ninety percent of people may start a story very simply but emphasis needs to be added at the outset to capture the audience. For example, see the two following examples:

Example 1

> *Today I was going to catch a flight to London, England. While waiting in the lounge, I saw a good friend of mine. We wound up catching up and managed to get seats next to each other.*

Example 2

> *Have you ever wondered just how small this world really is? We have instances and incidents all the time but do we really appreciate them. Today, I was going to catch a flight to London, England and while sitting in the lounge, I looked around and all of a sudden, I caught glimpse of someone I have not seen in ages and we had a great relationship in the past. I immediately went over and we had a lovely catch up. We wanted to carry our conversation on so we spoke to the agent at the gate and we managed to get seats next to each other...*

The real difference of Examples 1 and 2 is that Example 1 provides no focus and direction while Example 2 provides clear parameters about what the story is going to be about. Example 2 clearly outlines that the essence of the story is about how small the world really is and the importance of relationships.

The body of the story

This is where you set the scene and provide readers/listeners with vivid images through text. You want to bring the reader into your world using the five senses. Although you may be familiar with the basics of description; you need to share your thoughts as well. Use descriptors to strengthen that bridge between the reader/listener.

Using the airplane example from earlier, many of us have travelled by airplane and waited in the lounge before a flight. However, your reader may not have been on an airplane before and only seen similar images in a movie or television show. Remember to draw upon fundamental understanding and start adding pieces so the reader can fully appreciate your story; you want the reader/listener to feel like they are right next to you in that airport lounge.

Applying descriptors, expression and tone add volume to your story. You need to keep the body of your story robust so the reader has reasons to stay engaged. If you capture the interest, passion and enthusiasm, there is a good chance your reader/listener will be pulled into your story. If you believe in your story, it is going to be equally interesting for your reader/listener. If you cannot share in an interesting way, why would your reader be interested? Be aware of overwhelming your audience, you want a nice balance between substance and context. For example, you don't want to whisper at a rock concert or talk loudly during an opera. These are examples of how uncomfortable the setting would be if your interest and passion do not match the circumstances.

In addition, be cautious of using unnecessary words and descriptors just to add flare but not meaning to the story. Your story can become so long winded and adjective based that your reader may get turned off. I equate it to having too many desserts and then feeling overwhelmed by all the sugar.

Keep in mind your reader/listener is on this journey with you so be careful to balance length with content. It does not need to be an epic novel or a haiku. Talk the reader through the critical parts of the story by using descriptors but don't try to carry the story too long or its purpose and reason can be lost. Bollywood movies are notorious for this; they bring in multiple side stories and characters with no purpose or meaning so you are often left wondering why you were brought down that path in the first place. You need to guide your reader down the journey you are sharing.

Conclusion

Not all stories require a grand conclusion or a significant climactic finish. We would not have enough stories to tell if that was the case; everything would be in Hollywood style and the art of the conversation would be lost. The conclusion should restate purpose and importance of the story. Think about why you are telling the story and end on a note that the reader can understand and relate back to your introduction.

If your story has a casual setting and it is more of a conversation/discussion, keep your story shorter so you do not drag the conversation along. If you have something of significance to share, then make sure you craft an impactful ending where the reader can reflects on its meaning. Make sure the story does end and does not leave the reader/listener without a conclusion.

4) Apply and appeal to the senses of people

As human beings, we like to connect with each other. Whether it is verbally or in written form, we have an inherent need to connect. It could be over a meal in an intimate setting or in a small casual group. Stories are those descriptors and thoughts that add colour to our conversation.

For example, if you were with your co-workers and you said the following about a visit to an art exhibit:

"I went to an art exhibit by Philippe Halsman about famous people and it was good. Lots of greys but it also had some colour. My favorite image was of Albert Einstein."

Or

"Last night I went to a fantastic photo exhibit by Philippe Halsman; the photographer with this amazing sense of people. He captures images in black and white with intense detail. The images are unique because they hold warmth amidst the cool grey shades. One particular image that was my favorite was that of Albert Einstein. It captured the intensity of the man and in particular, his eyes. The depth of thought in his eyes were so captivating that you have to wonder what he was thinking of at the time. Halsman has sheer genius when it comes to using the camera to capture individual personalities on film."

Considering both descriptions, they describe a similar experience at a photo exhibit by Phillipe Halsman. The first description has very little content and just a brief descriptor. The second one provides additional detail about the exhibit and also focuses on one particular image that everyone can appreciate and understand. We can imagine seeing the shades of grey they are describing, the coldness of the image and the intensity. If we really try to appreciate the descriptions and close our eyes, we can use more of our senses to imagine the experience as described. The more sense and details provided in a story, the more the reader/listener can appreciate and relate to the experience.

An exercise to help you build on descriptors and imagery is to select an everyday object and expand on it. It could be as simple as a stone. Holding this in your hand, you might use words like, heavy, cold, hard, smooth, etc. Then taking each word, expand on it.

For example take the word 'heavy'. Holding the stone in my hand, I found it was rounded and worn. Expanding on heavy, I could describe it as dense and hefty in feel. If you were to throw it, it would make a loud crash or potentially break something.

Finally, be authentic. What this means is being genuine in your approach to storytelling. You need to have the credibility and authority. A person is not going to want to listen to your story if they don't believe in you.

How to be authentic? This takes time. Your character and reputation dictates how authentic you are. You need credibility to gain respect. Reflect on your stories and journey in an honest fashion, and then your verbal and written become the mechanism to share these reflections with others and gain respect. Respect is not gained instantly; it is something that happens over time. The importance of this cannot be understated, to be successful storyteller; you need your audience to appreciate who you are. You are your stories.

5) Remember your audience

Your stories may be very personal but it is the audience that will interpret meaning from it. While you are the individual telling the story, your listeners are the ones who will need to understand it. Not everyone will see the story through your lens. As individuals, we all bring our perceptions and attitudes to our interpretations. You may identify an important story from a specific event but someone else might see the incident in a completely different light. Perception is how we view the world through our own personal lens and can be impacted by our individual upbringing, culture, social identity and situational experiences. No two people have the same perceptions.

For example, if you ask someone, "You make ugly look beautiful." Is that a compliment or an insult? There is no right answer. I have asked this same question in a university class and I get mixed reactions and interpretations. For some, it means taking something distasteful and making it beautiful. Others interpret it to mean someone is not beautiful, but at the highest degree of ugly. I am always quite surprised by this because personally I equate this statement to be a compliment but that fits my outlook as I often view things in a positive light. If you viewed this comment in a more negative context, this does not mean you are a negative person; just your initial interpretation.

There will be instances where storytellers are disconnected from the audience. This does <u>not</u> mean you are a terrible storyteller. I reflect on the principle of 15/70/15. There will always be 15% of the audience on each side of the spectrum; 15% who really do not care about the story and 15% who are highly engrossed in everything you say. The remaining 70% fall along a spectrum from "it was interesting" to "that was fascinating and I would like to learn more". You cannot take somebody's disinterest personally. Your audience is a mix of people, ideas, thoughts and you will have some more interested audience members than others.

Even with this book, someone felt this section would be irrelevant to their storytelling because they were already highly reflective. Instead they considered Sections Two and Four to be more valuable because of the actual stories told.

Moving forward

So what does this all mean? This section provided insight into the foundation of storytelling. It started with the premise on what storytelling is and then shared a concept of how to discover the extraordinary in the ordinary concluding with some overarching concepts and ideas around the basics of what storytelling.

By establishing a strong foundation, you can start applying some of the principles we will be discussing. It is critical to look at storytelling as sharing your experience while understanding your audience. The audience will help guide your stories.

---

5 Key points that make up a good story
- Turn an incident into an experience
- Make sure it relates to the topic at hand
- Your story needs flow
- Apply and appeal to the senses of people
- Remember your audience

~ Quick Thoughts ~

PART TWO

"Four important 'C's to remember and helped in the creation of this book: When COMFORT replaces CHALLENGE, it is time to CHANGE by being CREATIVE." So when I started to feel comfortable, I needed to be challenged so I decided to change and become creative.
~ Sam Thiara

In a pearl necklace, each pearl is a unique component; formed from a particle of sand. My stories are no different, and when strung together, make a personal necklace of experiences. The common thread that holds each of my pearls in place is a chain fashioned out of my calm and reflective perspective. I take the time to understand the depth of my experiences and the significance it may hold.

I have built the ability to remain calm and reflective. Like a yogi master who is able to bend and move, I trained my mind to remain calm and collected rather than reactive and abrupt. We encounter a multitude of experiences every day and often view them in absolutes. When something happens, we often tell ourselves that it is good or bad and our experiences are shaped by the position we take. By dealing in absolutes, we take an immediate position and build from this perspective rather than considering the situation and assessing the impacts and possibilities.

For example, I often hear people complain about the rain in Vancouver. We get a lot of rain on the west coast of Canada and that is just a reality of our local climate. While at a café, customers often complain about the rain and how they wish they were somewhere else but that does not change the fact the rain will continue to fall. Personally, I tell myself that no matter how much it rains, it may dampen my clothes, but it will not dampen my spirit. When it rains, I approach activities differently. I dress appropriately and make the necessary changes to my original plan. I appreciate the sun but I have also learned to appreciate the rain. There is no need to be upset or bothered by something I cannot change.

Look at experiences by a different perspective. Think beyond the obvious and be creative and adaptable to what is provided. We can sit and wait for the perfect situation, but it may never come. Rather than focusing on what is wrong, try to look at what is possible.

Each story holds purpose and meaning and I often sit and interact with others and pull stories as they become applicable to the situation or discussion. Your stories define who you are and they make you unique. They are your experiences and a reflective mirror into your world. Through your descriptions and process, you can showcase to the world who you are. Your stories become you as you become your stories.

A Foundational Concept

In 2011, I was asked to deliver a TEDxSFU talk. I had 15 minutes to share a part of my life. With only 15 minutes and so much to say, I had to collect my thoughts on what I would be able to share. Like packing your luggage for a trip, I had to decide what items to keep and what to put back in the closet.

It was while I was in Cambridge, England on a train headed to London that I decided to come up with my presentation. Slowly my mind started to activate as I reflected on what I wanted share and it came to me. We live in the ordinary and embedded within the ordinary are tremendously extraordinary experiences.

I started jotting down bullet points and scribbled notes feverishly as my mind raced forward. By the end of the train ride, I had the foundation of my talk. I inserted my stories and shared it with a few people.

I credit one of my students, Angel Qi (she was an angel for me on this) for my concept. She commented, *"You have some great stuff here and I really like it and you tell great stories…but how can I tell stories?"* In a word, brilliant! I was so focused on the stories I had; I did not have that concept to share with the audience. I used her feedback to build an approach to help others share their stories. I broke down the steps that I take to formulate my stories and used it to establish a concept that became CARPE Diem. By embracing this, it has helped me to organize my thoughts and create a process that I can share with others.

CARPE Dicm

Carpe diem means seize the day or more accurately, 'pluck this day' and has been included in many influential speeches. The idea is that you need to live in the moment and undertake challenges and opportunities because the future is uncertain. In this case, carpe diem is also a great concept on how to build your personal stories. There is some relevance on seizing the moment and capturing it to build your personal story, but CARPE is now also an acronym for a process on how to build a story which I will share.

Often times, people think that stories need to be life altering or life changing to be interesting - the grand transition points in our lives. This is true and can result in some amazing stories that impact many people around us; however, stories can also be built out of the ordinary. It is about discovering the extraordinary in the ordinary.

Life is only ordinary if we think it is and do not realize the significant things embedded in the everyday. As you will see, CARPE is a tool that you can use to help 'you' find the extraordinary in the ordinary. Ordinary things and situations happen around us all the time, but we can make them extraordinary. For example, a simple set of footprints applied to CARPE, resulted in a compelling workshop on leadership and storytelling. If you take the letters CARPE and apply it into a process, you will be amazed at how this can help you.

CARPE stands for Curiosity, Appreciation, Reflection, Perspective and Experience

C – Curiosity – you need to go through life with a curious nature. Be aware and look for interesting things around you. Consider things from a different perspective than you normally would or review the obvious in a different light. This is the first part of the process where curiosity results in a conscious pause to look at something differently. The footprints in the sand caught my eye and I stopped to look about them more closely.

A – Appreciation – once you find something interesting, you need to appreciate it for more than its' initial impression. Appreciate situations, objects and people to help create meaning. Appreciation is a way of life where you build on the curiosity and attach significance to it. With appreciation, you start to think about things in greater detail. In the case of the footprints, I plopped myself down next to the footprints to really think about them.

R – Reflection – this is an important process because the 'C' and 'A' are helpful but only when you truly reflect on the significance, does it really matter. Reflection is the process of taking what you find and thinking beyond the obvious. Reflection is the maturation process you take for the things around us; you need to dedicate time to fully understand and appreciate it. As you reflect, you add deeper purpose and meaning. When I was appreciating the footprints, I needed to think further about them and add depth. The realization was that tomorrow the footprints are gone and how can I leave a lasting impression.

P – Perspectives – this is what you have accumulated over time. This is what makes up who you are and your view of the world. You find purpose and meaning once you can take the 'C' and 'A' and 'R' drive your thoughts forward and add your own personal meaning to it. Your perspectives impact how you process and create significance of the event, person or object. Whatever stopped you to think deeper, perspective adds dimension and elements to it. Your perspectives help you create unique purpose or meaning and others may interpret the same meaning or purpose very differently. While reflection helped me to realize an opportunity, perspective allowed me to create meaning towards the concepts so a foundation for a story could be formed. The footprints made me think about leaving a lasting impression; the perspectives added the content.

E – Experience – this is critical, once you have taken the four previous letters and pull it together, then you need to make it into an experience. An experience is something you catalogue for the future based on what happened. If you don't finalize it by capturing it as an experience, then the interaction dies an untimely death and is no longer a story. 'C', 'A', 'R', 'P', becomes a process to establish your story and the 'E' is what captures it and ties it all together. If you think about working on a puzzle and you have sections, the experiences are the various sections you are working on. The experience of finding the footprints provided a number of stories that emerged so that I could develop an entire workshop on how one can leave a lasting impression.

CARPE example – a doorstop becomes a leadership foundation
Here is another example to apply CARPE Diem to a real life situation that I encountered. I found a leadership concept and deeper meaning from a simple wooden wedge doorstop. Yes that is right, a wooden wedge doorstop! Something ordinary made extraordinary.

One day, I was walking from my car to my office and just as I was about to enter the building, I saw a wooden wedge doorstop by the door. There was nothing unique or special about it but I looked at it for an instant and instead of moving on, my 'C'uriosity kicked in. I had seen this doorstop before but I started to think about it differently. As I thought more and 'A'ppreciated it, I started to see more significance and meaning to it. Once I had fully considered and appreciated the function of the doorstop, I had walked ten minutes to my office and during that walk brought 'R'eflection into my thinking. I knew I had something but what did it mean? My 'P'erspective kicked in and made me ponder on a leadership concept derived from Sun Tzu.

Sun Tzu wrote the *Art of War* centuries ago as a manual for warfare. What was once used for warfare is now being used to fuel thoughts on leadership. One concept that always resonated with me from Sun Tzu's work was, "*A gentleman always keeps a sword by his side.*" This meant that I don't have to be a leader all the time but that I should have my 'sword' (leadership) by my side just in case I need to jump in and provide support and guidance. Once I am done, I can step back and wait for the next opportunity to use my sword. I can use my leadership when needed but when it is not, it can be sheathed. If you think about it, this is similar to the wooden doorstop because when needed it is kicked under the door to hold the door open. When it is not needed, it is tucked away, but available. The doorstop makes our lives easier, much like my leadership and is really no different than the sword by my side.

Now you get an extra concept from the door stop. We often say, "*When opportunity knocks, we have to go through the door.*" Well, that doorstop is what keeps the door open for us so we can go through. This refers to the people in our lives who open doors for us. It also means we need to find the wooden doorstops in our lives to help us prop that door open. Just do not call them a door stop.

This is where the 'E' is important; to take the concept of the doorstop and make it a meaningful 'E'xperience, I need to build it into one of my own personal incidents. In this case, the experience is realizing that there are a few thoughts:

- Something as simple as a doorstop can have an important leadership concept attached to it.
- We have many obvious objects and situations around us. There is an opportunity to be able to build significance around it.
- CARPE Diem can be a valuable method of trying to find the extraordinary in the ordinary.

Let me recap the doorstop situation to demonstrate the steps.

- Curiosity – stopped me when I saw the doorstop
- Appreciation – made me realize that this is more than a doorstop but was not sure what
- Reflection – As I was walking to my office, I thought deeper on what the doorstop meant to me
- Perspective – By adding my personal perspectives, I was able to pull Sun Tzu's concept to my situation and apply the principle
- Experience – By cataloging this incident as an experience, I was able to capture this story and be able to share with others

Another quick example to share about the significance of CARPE and how you can find significance around you. Recently, I met my good friend Rick Antonson and he is retiring after many years at Tourism Vancouver as the President and CEO. Over the years, we have forged a lifelong friendship and he has been instrumental in helping me shape this book. When I have been to Rick's office, there are many globes that sit on his shelf that relate to his world. I gave Rick a special retirement gift that is related to a globe, I gave him an old brass compass. The reason for the compass is that I see Rick more as a compass who guides and supports others than a globe. He will not take you to the destination but will merely point you in the direction. That is his leadership and fitting as a gift. To come up with this gift, I went through CARPE and each step and it led me to this initiative.

Use CARPE Diem to look for objects, events and people that provide purpose and meaning in your life. Look beyond the obvious and start appreciating things as they emerge and make sure to capture it and record it. What if you looked at a light bulb, what is beyond the light bulb? How about a garbage bin? Sure it holds trash but what concept can you pull to add meaning to it?

Action:

Take an object, person or situation and think about it from a different perspective. Apply the concept of CARPE Diem to try and build a meaningful story around it. Try using the CARPE part as a process. The exercise can be something that has happened in the past or to randomly take an object, person or situation and seeing what you can pull as meaning. Take each letter and draw upon them and write a sentence or paragraph. For example (and don't be limited by the following):

- *A child or pet playing*
- *The key to a car*
- *Sitting in a coffee shop and looking at the people inside with you or outside the window*
- *An empty cup*
- *Go to the park or beach and look at the ground, what do you see?*

To help you better appreciate CARPE Diem, there is a breakdown for each letter and a story that I share to help formulate the process. Each story demonstrates the strength of each letter but what you will notice is that each story has CARPE as a process. These are five foundational stories that have been important in my life and I needed to share. They include important people, situations and things.

CARPE – Process to build your story

- Curiosity - stop
- Appreciation - enjoy
- Reflection - think
- Perspective - views
- Experience - recall

<u>C</u>ARPE Diem- Curiosity

> **Curiosity -** cu·ri·os·i·ty - [kyoo r-ee-os-i-tee]
> noun, plural cu·ri·os·i·ties.
> 1. the desire to learn or know about anything; inquisitiveness.
> 2. a <u>curious</u>, rare, or novel thing.
> **3. a strange, <u>curious</u>, or interesting quality.**

This is the foundation of personal storytelling and how you start discovering the extraordinary in the ordinary. Go through life with an inquisitive nature and understand that there are adventures around you at all times. You literally have to switch your radar on and anticipate that you will encounter opportunities and they might not be in the most obvious ways.

Curiosity can be unconventional and that is what makes it interesting. It is about looking at the ordinary in life with an understanding that there might be another interesting way to experience it and questioning the obvious. It might be thinking about an object in a different way or speaking to someone and sparking an engaging conversation. By going through life with a curious nature, you start capturing ideas and thoughts.

Curiosity paid off in a big way a few years back when I sparked a random conversation and wound up making a very close friend for life.

A Train Ride that Changed My Life
In 2006, I started working on my Master's degree in Leadership Studies at the University of Exeter in Devon, England. Imagine a person in their mid-40's standing about to leave from the train station in Southampton to get to their university class and their aunt points and says, *"Don't talk to strangers!"* Really? Am I six years old? Even though I was an adult, my aunt was worried someone would take advantage of me. As you will see, I did not heed her advice.

While I was on the train from Southampton to Exeter, I spoke to a couple of passengers in passing but nothing meaningful. I arrived, attended my class and took a train to London and then to Cambridge to meet a former student of mine, Sarah, who was studying in Cambridge. I changed at the

Kings Cross station and chose one of the multiple cars at random and sat down, the train was not overly full.

I unfolded a tourist map to locate my hotel; the map showed the train station and the hotel but I had no idea of how far the distance in-between was. I asked a passing conductor for some help and he said, *"Sorry mate, don't live in Cambridge so can't help you out,"* and then proceeded on in a very brisk manner. A few seconds passed and then a gentleman across the aisle commented, *"Sorry, I just heard you were trying to find how far your hotel is from the station and I live in Cambridge. Perhaps I can help."* I showed him the map and he said, *"Looking at your luggage, distance and you, it is far but you can do it."*

This is where the story could have ended if I thanked him, put my headphones on and let life pass me by (like many people do), but this was not the case. Instead, I kept conversing with this stranger and even commented on his British and North American accent. He explained that he was born in India, spent his life in the United States and then he had lived in Cambridge for the last 10 years. Through our conversation, I told him how I was starting my leadership studies and that brought me to England. I then found out he was teaching at Cambridge and was a professor of leadership studies. That was the field I was just starting to work on and here was an expert! What are the chances that you would wind up sitting with someone who had such a similar background? We had the most enjoyable conversation all the way up to Cambridge.

When it came time to go our separate ways, he provided me with his address and phone number and asked me to pay him a visit, which I did. We shared in each other's company and stories and talked about life. I learned much about him and he learned much about me. A chance meeting on a train, led to shared stories and a strong level of trust and friendship between us. We have kept in touch and visited each other over the years. He travels around the world, teaching and consulting on leadership and has expressed interest in collaborating with me on a future project. I am often amazed at how we met, how we have stayed connected and how we have become like brothers.

I have recounted this story to hundreds of people and each time, I reflect on our chance meeting. What if I sat in another car, or if I sat at the other end of the train? Perhaps we would never have met. It was a chance encounter that I am very grateful for. I wonder how many times we have all overlooked a person like this in our life just because we were not curious to ask a question or aware of the situation. This is not the first time this has happened to me in my life. I have made countless lifelong friends along the way. If either of us were not curious or open to engaging in conversation with a stranger, we would not have formed such a strong relationship.

Curiosity is about asking questions, discovering and being open to new adventures. If you take the concept of CARPE Diem and the 'C' as curiosity, you can see how both of us were open enough to ask and pursue a relationship. Curiosity is what started the spark of this life long relationship.

Action:

- *Based on this story and in your own words, how would you describe curiosity?*

- *Think about a time in the past when you were curious or wanted to know about something or someone. Can you think why you were curious and why it was important? What is it about your incident that sparked thoughts of a curious nature?*

- *Now that you have a grasp and understanding of curiosity, start walking around and looking at the world through a different lens. Start thinking about things differently than the obvious and talk to strangers and ask questions. Look for the deeper understanding and meaning of things by starting to be curious about the world around you. Here is a simple exercise. Take an object, any object around you and try to write down as many things about that object you can imagine and think about. Go beyond the boundary of what the object is and start to vision more than what it is.*
  - *Object observed:*
  - *What colour is it?*
  - *What other objects have other colours like this object?*
  - *What do you notice that is unique about this object?*
  - *If you had to describe this object to someone who has never seen it, what would you say about it so they can picture it*

CARPE Diem- Appreciation

> **Appreciation -** ap·pre·ci·a·tion
> [Uh-pree-shee-ey-shuh n]
> noun
> 1. gratitude; thankful recognition: They showed their appreciation by giving him a gold watch.
> 2. clear perception or recognition, especially of aesthetic quality: a course in <u>art</u> appreciation.
> 3. critical notice; evaluation; opinion, as of a situation, person, etc.

2

If curiosity is the start of story building, appreciation is the next step. Once something has been identified as interesting or out of the ordinary, you need to appreciate it for more than the obvious. Appreciation is looking at something in a different light and then accepting it for more than what it's perceived worth is. It is an expression of gratitude for a person, situation or object. If curiosity sparked my conversation with a complete stranger on the train, appreciation is what took it further.

The following is an example of appreciation as the result of a life altering experience. Every day we get up, go to school or work and then we come home and go to bed, only to repeat this routine again the next day. Seconds turn to minutes, minutes into hours, hours into days, days into months, and months into years and before you know it, you are looking back at your life and wondering what you could have done differently. We settle into comfort and routine. In this situation, we accept consistency and shy away from change. For many, life can feel mechanical. Sometimes we don't realize how precious our lives are or understand some of the simple things that are around us. We go to work with the assumption that all is well, life is fine and then something triggers a rude awakening. Do not take the everyday for granted.

How Life Changes – Tragedy to Appreciation

On February 10, 1972 and I was almost 10 years old. Like any other day, I woke up, got ready, and went to school. It was just a typical day, but still vivid in my memory. I came home after school and saw my aunt was there. This was not uncommon as she only lived a few houses away. After a cup of tea, she told me that my father was in an accident. I did not see this as a serious situation; I thought he had rolled into a ditch and that he would be home later that afternoon. To this day, I still have this image of his car rolling into a ditch, him getting out and then walking home. My mind created this image because nobody gave me any other details of what actually happened. Without realizing how wrong I was, I went out to play with my friends. Later that evening, my dad had not come home and my mom was nowhere to be seen. I thought that this was odd. My mom came home about 9PM and I noticed something was wrong. Now I was concerned.

It turned out that there was an industrial accident at my father's workplace. The cable on the elevator my father was in along with two others had fallen three floors. One person fractured his hip, the other fractured his skull and both would eventually recover. We had no idea about the extent of my father's injuries. Two days later I was permitted to see him in hospital and it was a sight I will never forget. They had him strapped into a metal bed and every so often the nurses would come in and flip him over – bed and all. I then learned that the injuries were significant and that he would never walk again. His legs and spine had shattered in the accident and he was now a paraplegic. At almost 10 years old, you have difficulty saying paraplegic let alone understanding what it means. All I knew was that he would never walk again.

He went to work that cold winter morning in February and almost never came home. In an instant, our lives had changed drastically. I remember seeing his work boots at home, the ones he wore that day. They were a constant reminder about how you go to work one day and then everything changes in a flash. My family was feeling despair, fear and concern because we were now in the unknown. You went from being a kid to a kid who now has to be responsible.

Without knowing it, our lives changed drastically in a matter of seconds. Life is precious, time is precious and you must be sure to use it wisely. I realized at a very young age that there are no guarantees in life and since then, walking out every morning, I treasure and embrace anything and everything because I am not sure when it will be over for me. This is not a morbid thought but one of finding purpose and meaning and this became my foundation of appreciation.

The story does have a happy ending, our lives turned out fine. My father is still a paraplegic, but that has never stopped our family from enjoying life to the fullest. In fact, it brought our family closer together and I feel we have done more together than your average family. Our lives would have been considerably different if February 10, 1972 would have been a normal day, but I owe a lot to my father. He has taught me that it is more about what you can do versus what you cannot do. I see how he has kept his outlook on life positive and his attitude has strengthened me as a person.

I remember one person commenting how tragic it was to have my father go through the ordeal and then being confined in a wheelchair. When I shared that we never saw it as good or bad, that person felt it was insensitive to not view it as negative. My perspective is that we cannot change what happened. Life dealt us a hand and it is how we chose to handle it that helped us move forward. It is neither good nor bad, it happened and we needed to move on. If you dwell on less fortunate incidents, it is sure to weigh you down like an anchor. If tragedy hits and life changes, try to understand what this means. It is difficult at times because we can easily find negativity in such situations. Instead, I choose not to dwell or be negative about it. Instead, I look at these events as life lessons and move on to appreciate life for all that it holds and brings.

Life altering situations can be both tragic and/or glorious. I have also had many positive life altering moments such as getting married, having two children, graduating from school, working on amazing projects, writing this book, going on a year long journey and many more significant occurrences. Each one brings up powerful thoughts and emotions.

It reminds me of a saying that I read almost every day to live to the fullest:

"This is the beginning of a new day. You have been given this day to use as you will. You can waste it or use it for good. What you do today is important because you are exchanging a day of your life for it... A DAY OF YOUR LIFE... When tomorrow comes, this day will be gone forever; in its place is something that you have left behind... let it be something good."
~ Anonymous

I appreciate each and every day that I am allowed to be on this earth. I appreciate each and every person I come in contact with. I appreciate each and every thing I do.

Every morning, I have a choice, and I tell myself that I will appreciate all that the day holds because I have no idea when it will end. I am grateful for the extraordinary in the ordinary. I think the best way to understand this concept is that I choose how I will react to a situation and will not have the situation rule me. It is about taking control and deciding I need to pull on the positive. Every night I go to bed, I think to myself that I had an amazing day and wait for tomorrow's adventure.

Appreciation is an important piece of personal storytelling because it provides the personal substance and passion so that you add purpose and meaning.

Action:

- *After reading this piece, what are some of the things you pulled from the story that demonstrates appreciation?*
- *What are some of the things you are grateful for? Who are some of the people you appreciate. Write down what/who and why.*
- *Have you had something that has changed your life? If so, how did it impact you and how did you feel. If it is negative, what are some of the positive aspects you can pull from it that you might not have thought about?*

CA<u>R</u>PE Diem - Reflection

Reflection - re·flec·tion -[ri-flek-shuh n]

noun

1. the act of reflecting or the state of being reflected.
2. an <u>image</u>; representation; counterpart.
3. a fixing of the thoughts on something; careful consideration.
4. a thought occurring in consideration or meditation.

3

Once you have identified something due to curiosity and now appreciated it for more than what it is worth, it is only through reflection that you start to create deeper purpose and meaning and add more significance. Reflection is the piece that allows your thoughts to mature. This is the difficult part of adding to the curiosity and appreciation. What does it all mean? The journey has started with curiosity and appreciation but where is it leading? Reflection helps to answer the questions.

By nature, I am a reflective person and consider things from many areas and perspectives. My reflective sense has developed over time and over many instances and incidents. Reflection for storytelling does not happen in an instant but rather it develops and grows over time. You may be curious about something and appreciate it, but as you think about it over time and reflect on an incident, you add more substance to it. Through reflection you draw upon multiple areas and start to pull different parts of your life puzzle together.

An example of reflection and resulting realization emerged from a year long journey and a hacker. This story provides a perspective that one can adopt to consider situations and occurrences in a different perspective than the obvious good or bad.

Hacker help

Earlier in the book I spoke about a year long and epic journey. I was turning 50 years old in 2012 and in October 2011 my wife started asking what I wanted to do to recognize this milestone. She had envisioned a large scale party, but that was not what I wanted. I started to think about the year and what it should hold and decided I wanted to create a blog called – *Sam's 50/50-2012*. I was going to blog about the extraordinary in the ordinary from January 1-December 31, 2012 and on January 1, 2013, I was going to list the 50 most memorable things about turning 50. I encourage you to embrace this idea and do a 30/30 birthday or a 5/5 anniversary. Make it whatever you want it to be; because it can be such a memorable journey!

One of the students I mentored, Will, self-taught himself the skills and created the blog. With the help of another person, Connie, the site went live on January 1, 2012. *Sam's 50/50-2012* (http://sams50-50.com/) was born and a year long journey started. I credit much of this project, and my writing voice, to these two individuals. I got the opportunity to do some amazing things and through reflection, found significance in the everyday things. Every blog post had come out of reflection.

In November 2012, I was about one month away from completing this journey and at the 89th blog post for the year; I received an email from my contributing author, Adam. He said I should check out my website as he thought a hacker had compromised it. Sure enough, all the content was gone, and replaced with a note 'hacked by hacker'. My site was down! I was very frustrated at first and like many of you, I logged onto Facebook and updated my status. Getting that out of the way, I was not going to give up. I did not just spend almost a year to get this close and not complete the journey.

All of a sudden, my students came to my aid and showed me how I might recover some of the cache. I also had some blog posts in a saved document. I started the difficult task of meticulously piecing my blog together in chronological order. It was like having a porcelain vase break into many pieces and trying to glue it all back together. While trying to recover from this setback, I was thinking about everything that had happened. Eventually, I pulled all the documents and blog posts together and realized I had about 94 pages and 30,000 words of content. I might have an instant book here! It was through reflection that I originally authored these blogs and it was through reflection and considering my situation that I realized I had enough material for a book if I choose to. I will not thank the hacker because their intentions were far from honourable; however, through adversity, this person has helped me to come up with another book idea.

The story does not end there. Will and Connie met with me and like something out of a movie, Connie was able to restore the site so I could go on and complete the journey and on January 1, 2013. I felt like the athlete that stumbled, got back up and crossed the finish line of an epic marathon.

There are situations that happen all around us; it is only through thinking about them and reflecting that you start to consider things from another perspective. The obvious and easiest reaction would have been for me to throw my hands in the air and walk away. Instead, I took the time to consider what had happened and looked at options. Sometimes options are not obvious and need to be uncovered. If I thought linearly, my conclusion was to give up. Instead I thought more abstractly and considered additional options through reflection and discovered a new path that was not visible previously.

A friend told me once:

There is greatness in 'pushing at the edges' of what you know yourself to be capable of. If you're not failing, you're probably playing small. If you have failures on a regular basis, you're playing in the ever-expanding boundary area of what you're capable of as a human being. Too many people "play small" in life, which is really too bad. I'd rather be "playing a big game in life", or really swinging for the fences - to use a baseball analogy, even if there are failures.

I'd rather have big problems than little problems. If my biggest "problem" is picking the outfit I'm going to wear when I wake up in the morning, I probably am not going to put an end to world hunger, end homelessness, or cure cancer in the afternoon. I draw a parallel here to your email signature about making yours an interesting autobiography. Would you like your tombstone to read "Always wore matching clothes to the office" or "Had a well decorated apartment?"

I always choose the more difficult road because it is less crowded than the obvious path.

Action:
After reading this, hopefully you recognize that through reflection, you can pull deep purpose and meaning from your experiences. In this case, it was finding acceptance from a situation that might not have been favorable.

Think about a time when you had an incident occur, which you felt was not so favorable.
- *Can you look at it from a different perspective and see a deeper meaning than you had before?*
- *Consider a situation in your life and start reflecting on it and lay out as many option alternatives as you can think of – realistic or not, just list them out.*
- *Now after examining all the facts, is there anything you can draw from this that might help to look at it from a different perspective?*
- *This is likely the most difficult part because you might not see things right away, you can always put thoughts and ideas on the shelf for later examination.*

Perspectives - per·spec·tive - [per-spek-tiv]

noun

1. a technique of depicting volumes and spatial relationships on a flat surface. Compare <u>aerial perspective</u>, <u>linear perspective</u>.
2. a picture employing this technique, especially one in <u>which</u> it is prominent: an architect's perspective of a house.
3. a visible scene, especially one extending to a distance; vista: a perspective on the main axis of an estate.
4. the state of existing in space before the eye: The elevations look all right, but the building's composition is a failure in perspective.
5. the state of one's ideas, the facts known to one, etc., in having a meaningful interrelationship: You have to live here a few years to see local conditions in perspective.

4

Curiosity, appreciation and reflection will only get you so far. Perspectives are the accumulation of experiences, thoughts and ideas that we use to find significance in the incidents around us. We have formed our perspectives over time through stories, interactions, school, and media. These become our beliefs, truths, views of the world and we draw upon these to find purpose and meaning. It is an entire filing cabinet of experiences, or in more modern terms, countless gigabytes of storage. Your perspectives are likely different than mine. If there are a single set of footprints in the sand and I can find purpose and meaning behind them, what do you draw from footprints, perhaps a different meaning or perhaps not.

Perspectives are generated by us. It is everything we are exposed to in this world that shapes who we are. The following is an example to draw upon that demonstrates how perspective provided a life altering view of the world.

Can I change the world? Yes I did and so can you!

There are times in our life where we feel small and insignificant. I often hear people say that they want to make meaningful change but that it is too large or complicated and can they really make a difference? Should they even bother? We tell ourselves that there are so many needs out there and we possibly can't make a difference. Where do we even start?

What if I told you that you have already made significant impacts that have literally changed the world? It really is about seeing it from a different perspective.

When I was 16 years old, I had a lofty vision that I was going to change the world. Don't know when, don't know how, but I was going to change the world. The older I got the more distant the vision became to where it almost vanished and I was somewhat disappointed that I did not accomplish this goal.

Many years later, I did a nine month leadership program through Leadership Vancouver. This was a fascinating organization because it was not focused leadership theory but rather its real world application in the community. There are two types of people that entered Leadership Vancouver; those who were already engaged in the community and wanted to expand their outreach and those who did not know where to start and were looking for the avenues to make a difference. I fell into the second category. If you looked at my resume before Leadership Vancouver, it was very light with community involvement and leadership. The program also reinforced that I had a purpose to work towards with the betterment of the community and re-ignited the aspect of making a difference.

Upon graduation, I sat next to a fellow named David from the Harvest Project. He proceeded to tell me how he was the Executive Director of an organization that was working to get people off income assistance. I was taken by their motto, *'Offering a hand up not a hand out.'* David talked about their clients who were unemployed and trying to find their break in life. He needed someone to do resumes, resume writing workshops and interview skills workshops. I finally found a project to dedicate my efforts and find purpose.

With enthusiasm I started to help the clients with their resumes on a one on one basis. I worked on over 100 resumes during my involvement with the Harvest Project but the ones that stand out were the eighth and ninth resumes. These two resumes belonged to a couple who recently moved to North Vancouver, living in a one room bachelor suite with their 8 year old daughter who slept on the floor. The gentleman told me how his world was collapsing around him because he could not provide for his family, he did not know what to do and he didn't see a future for his daughter. We talked at length about how to see things from a new perspective and to search out opportunities. How we try to find someone to rescue us but at times we need to look within ourselves to rescue ourselves. After our conversation, I completed their resumes and dropped them off at the Harvest Project. The difficulty with working on a project like this is that you rarely find out how things turn out because the clients pick up the resume at their convenience and go on with their lives. So you just hope for the best.

A few years later, I happened to be visiting our local police detachment for a board meeting. While I was waiting for the Sergeant, I saw a familiar face; it was the gentlemen from the Harvest Project. He came up to me and said, *"Sam, I am not sure if you know who I am?"* I replied that I remembered helping him and his wife with their resumes. It turns out that after our meeting, he used the new resume and proceeded to continue his job search with renewed enthusiasm. What resonated with him and his wife the most about our discussion was the ability to rescue themselves. Their perspective had changed; they realized nobody was going to swoop in to rescue them. Instead of waiting for a rescuer, they needed to find enablers and champions to help them get where they needed to go.

Shortly after our first meeting, he landed a government contract and was doing well, he could now provide for his family and his daughter had a future again. They moved in a larger home and their daughter now had her own room. What was most significant to me was that he described how his 'world' had come back together. As he said that, it suddenly hit me and hit me hard! Here I was trying to change the world through my eyes but I realized that it is actually more about the things I do to help others. Through my actions to make a difference in their lives, I could change the world they saw. I didn't think my actions were significant at the time, but through this person's eyes, his world had changed significantly. Through simple actions and helping where we can, we <u>can</u> change the world for others. By being a champion and enabler, we can make meaningful change, one person at a time.

It is all about perspectives. I think what was most significant for me was that maybe I was doing this all wrong. Maybe my life's journey was not to change the world as <u>I</u> saw it, but by impacting the lives of others I could change the world the way <u>they</u> saw it.

This story has had a profound impact on my life because I now share with others how they can change the world by impacting others. I still hold on to my dream of making an impact in the world and while I do that, I will carry on trying to change the world through the eyes of others – one person at a time

Perspective was important to this story because it helped me to provide insight to this couple through lengthy discussions. Perspective was also a tool that helped me see there was a new way to look at the world we live in. We each possess unique perspectives on how things are, and should be. We need to tap into our perspectives to help us assess situations and become the catalyst for change. Change starts with us. You possess a unique set of perspectives and thoughts that you is a valuable resource. You would be amazed at what you can do when you put your mind to it.

Action:

- *Make a list of the places where you think your perspective emerges from. What are the sources?*
- *After reading this piece, what are some of the things you have done that you can now realize might have had a profound impact on others?*
- *Has this changed your perspectives? If so, how?*
- *What can you try to do in the future that might open the eyes of others and allow you to now make a difference in the world?*

CARP**E** Diem – Experience

Experience - ex·pe·ri·ence - [ik-speer-ee-uh ns]

noun

1. a particular instance of personally encountering or undergoing something: My encounter with the <u>bear</u> in the woods was a frightening experience.
2. the process or fact of personally observing, encountering, or undergoing something: business experience.
3. the observing, encountering, or undergoing of things generally as they occur in the course of time: to learn from experience; the range of human experience.
4. knowledge or practical wisdom gained from what one has observed, encountered, or undergone: a man of experience.
5. Philosophy . the totality of the cognitions given by perception; all that is perceived, understood, and remembered.

5

The final piece to storytelling and building your story is taking the previous four elements we discussed; curiosity, appreciation, reflection and perspective and capturing the context of the elements and making it into an experience. This means permanently cataloguing the incident or occurrence for the future. If you do not capture the essence of your story as an experience then it will never become a story because it cannot be recounted.

Curiosity sparked the interest, appreciation made you seek deeper meaning; reflection helped you to add depth, and perspective allowed you to engage yourself fully into the situation. Experience is the final aspect that allows you to capture all the elements together for labelling and cataloguing.

The following example is an experience I had that I can share in story. It showcases persistence in the face of challenge and provides some valuable life lessons.

In Search of My Roots – A Village Far Away

Anything worth pursuing in life means being persistent and overcoming obstacles; it is also about focusing your attention to the task at hand and seeing actions through to completion. Unfortunately, people around you may not agree and will say a goal is too lofty or not worth pursuing. Why waste your time on something that you might not accomplish? In the end, it comes down to how persistent you are in pursuit of your goal. If there is anything you want to accomplish or achieve, you are destined to accomplish it until you create limitations. I often advise university students that if there is a job they want, a career they want to pursue or a company they envision themselves becoming a part of, they are on a crash course to accomplish this as long as they don't limit themselves. The journey can be difficult as they need to be committed, focused and find the right champions and time to accomplish their goals but not impossible.

A few years ago, I wanted to visit India for the first time to seek out my family's origins and find our ancestral village. That might sound strange to many because I am of Indo-Canadian heritage so the first assumption is that I am from India and the second one is that I have family there. My grandfather left the Punjab and India in the late 1800's and found his way to the Fiji Islands. There he started his life and family.

Growing up in Canada during the 60's and 70's, there was not a lot of Indo-Canadians to connect with and I was more interested in the usual things a growing boy would appreciate including hockey, friends and hanging out. When I asked my father about our roots and there were only three things he could tell me. He would say that my grandfather would write letters to Garhshankar (which was 5 miles from the village) and that our village name is Chhaduari in Hoshiarpur.

Years later, people would say, *"You are mistaken, there is no village named Chhaduari to speak of, it must be something else."* Another group of people cautioned that if I went in search of my village in India, people may think I am there for a land claim and would not be welcomed. Others wondered why it was so important to me. I started to feel that this was going to be a difficult task since I had very limited information, not the best of sources to work from and not so helpful people around me. Why was this important to me? Let me address that later.

I attempted to conduct some research and asked around for information but was not successful. My father's older brother had been to our village a few times, but he passed away 20 years earlier from when I initiated this search. There was nobody else who had the information I desperately needed to find the village and my grandfather's home. My father's oldest brother's son (my cousin) was too young to remember and my aunt in England thought she had a lead with someone from our village. All avenues were turning cold but I was determined. The noise around me continued as people questioned why I was trying to find the village and the reception I would receive. I decided that I would cross that bridge, if and when those challenges presented themselves.

 Two days before I was to leave for India, I received a letter from my cousin in California who was able to find a photo my uncle had taken of the people in our village. The day before I flew out, I received an email from a step-cousin in Fiji who said that he made it to Garhshankar but could not find our village. He said that the village name was Janodi. I now started to feel that I had some solid leads. I looked up Janodi on the Internet with no luck, but there was a village named Jandoli that was 5 miles from Garhshankar. Chhadauri or Jandoli, if you say them fast, they sound very similar, especially when repeated over and over.

I thought that over the years, the village name from Chhaduari could be interpreted as Jandoli. I mean it has been many years since we had any connection back to the village. Information can change over time and the names were somewhat similar sounding. Armed with this information and the photograph I was off on my adventure. It felt like it was all a puzzle and some of the important pieces were still missing but these might come forward as we worked towards it.

On a cold November day, my wife and I embarked on a personal journey to India with a photo, a journal to record my journey and a lot of hope. First, we visited the Golden Temple in Amritsar, which is the holiest of all places for Sikhs. I took the time and spiritual surroundings to think through what I was going to do if I found my family's village and what to do if I did not find it. I had come a long way and doubts started surfacing around what people were telling me and how it was going to be difficult. I quickly put those thoughts aside and embraced the moment.

After our time at the Golden Temple, we started looking for my village from Jalandhar (a city about 35 miles away from Garhshankar), and we went straight to Jandoli. Jandoli was easily found on the map and when we arrived, we found people sitting around in a compound. Imagine a stranger showing up to your house with a photo and asking if you are part of their family. That is what we did, we showed them the photo and they did not recognize the house, but they thought they recognized someone in the photo. Two people got into our truck to help us find that person and we were off. In my journal, I wrote about how my anticipation was building as I got another clue towards finding my family. When we arrived to the house, ten people gathered around to look at the picture and we quickly determined that this was not the right place. However, they did recognize someone in the photo. Two more people got into our truck and we were off again. We got to another house, another 10 people gathered around us and then we determined it was the wrong house and two new people got into our truck.

Everyone seemed to understand my plight and need to discover my roots and went out of their way to help. I soon realized that the information I had was not accurate and finding my village was not going to be easy.

Jandoli had lovely people, but it was the wrong village. I was disappointed as we returned to Jalandhar and our hotel. I felt like a climber who got so close to the summit of Everest and was forced to turn around due to inclement weather. This was my Everest and at every step, I felt like I was about to be turned around without reaching the summit. My fundamental problem was with the information I had or lack of it. At this point in my journey, I called my parents in Canada. They were proud of my attempt and advised there was no shame in not being able to locate the village as I was trying my best. Underlying, I could sense the sadness in their voices.

Why was this so important to me? Well, I realized that no one else in my family was going to attempt this journey and I realized that if I did not find this village and it skipped another generation, it would be lost forever. An even more important reason was that my father sacrificed so much for us and I knew he would not be able to travel to our village, so I needed to find it for him.

The next day we decided not to give up and try once more. It was time to go to basics and see what we could find. If this attempt would not work, then I would be heading home without any answers. I informed our driver of the plans to head to Garhshanker and to ask people and see what might emerge.

We got to Garhshankar and we started asking the locals about Chhaduari. Too our surprise and amazement, a couple of the locals advised us that was about five to six miles up a certain road. I had reserved enthusiasm as we headed to our destination and I wrote in my journal – *'Here we go again'*. We got to the entrance of this village and saw an old man sitting there. Our driver approached him and started talking to him and showed the photograph from 25 years ago. The old man thought that the house looked familiar and said that we should go up a certain roadway. He got into our truck, and like previous times, we wound up at a house that looked much different than the photo. At this point, I was writing in my journal that we are in Chhaduari and off to another house. I was guarded with my hope at this point.

While we waited in our truck, a few more people came out and discussions took place. A female elder was shown the photograph and after carefully examining the photo, she pointed and to our surprise said, *"That's me...that's me in the photo!!"* We had reached the right place! My heart was racing as I realized that this was the destination, this was my village, and this was my house and my people! My journal entry was simple and succinct, *"We found it!!!"*

The elder was named Prakash Kaur and after she realized where we came from and who I was, she gave me a big hug and started to weep. I showed her a photo of my dad's older brother and before I could say anything, she said, *"This is Ranjit Singh. Whatever happened to him because he never came back?"* I told her that he passed away over 20+ years ago and she suddenly became silent. She did not realize that he had died.

I shared photos of my family in Canada and explained who all the people were. I asked a number of questions and how we were all related. People now ask how close the relationship in the village is. The family I met were my grandfather's brother's family (my grand uncle's family). They knew about all the relationships in my family.

I now have a family tree along with the address and phone number of our village. One reason why it was difficult to find the village was that I was always told that our village was in the District of Hoshiarpur. It turns out that years ago, Hoshiarpur was too large so the authorities created a neighbouring district of Nawanshehar. We had the right name of the village but the wrong district. My new found family wanted us to stay longer but we could not due to our limited time. In the time we did have, my village family took us around and showed us the village and the fields, we shared a meal, and sat and enjoyed each other's company. We are 2,000 strong and I got the opportunity to see where my grandfather was from. I was overwhelmed and overjoyed.

Knowing that my father would not be able to travel to the village, I was determined to find the village and bring it to him. So much so that I went out to the fields and put a handful of dirt in zip lock bag to share with my father. Sure, I went to India and all my father got was a bag of dirt, but it was good dirt; it was a piece of our roots!

On our way out, my family told us to come back soon or at least in a couple of years for a village wedding. As we drove away, I felt like I was leaving a part of me behind. It is difficult to describe the feeling but it was an overwhelming sense of accomplishment. As our car drove away, it started to rain and we were told that it was a blessing. With a smile on my face and new photos of my family I was heading back to Jalandhar.

A couple of days later I was spoke to my father in Vancouver and told him that I had found the village. The enthusiasm went around the room and unknown to me, the word spread throughout my family in Canada and to relations around the world. I did not realize that people thought I had taken on a huge task with a low chance of success. Once I found it, people had a renewed sense of wanting to visit the pind (village) and learn more about our history.

This is an epic life story that had challenges, obstacles, enthusiasm, passion and finally success. I have to admit that I am glad that it was a difficult challenge. How interesting would this story have been if I got off the plane and drove to the village and met the family? Likely it would be much shorter and a much less interesting encounter to share.

If I had not recorded it and detailed it as an experience, this would not be a compelling story. I captured the emotions and details to develop the experience and make it significant. Now it has become story that I share with audiences on the topic of persistence. We all need to look back and capture all the stories we have held on to and revive them so they are not forgotten. Moving forward, start embracing events while they happen, turn the situation into an experience so it too becomes a memorable story.

Why was this story so important to me? There are a number of reasons:

- I realized that if I did not find the village on this trip we would skip another generation and make it that much more difficult if not impossible the next time. The chances of finding my family's origins diminished with each year that passed by. I found out that Prakash Kaur passed away a couple of years ago, without her I would not have realized I had found the right village.
- A sense of learning where my family roots are from. It is a grounding feeling to know that this is where generations of our ancestors originate from.

- When someone tells me that something is difficult or that I should not bother, this story strengthens my determination to achieve it.
- People thought finding the village was impossible, but that if someone could, that would be me because I always love a good challenge.

Activity:
Think about something you wanted to pursue.
- *Write down some of the reasons you pursued it.*
- *Write down some of the reasons that emerged from people about why they thought it was not worth pursuing.*
- *What steps did you take to move forward?*
- *Is there a goal you are considering?*
- *What do you think you might do to pursue it and stay persistent?*

Think about something you want to pursue.
- *What is your goal?*
- *Why is it important to you?*
- *What do you need to do to help you start going along the journey to realize this goal?*
- *Who do you need to include in your goal?*

Thoughts about CARPE

As you have seen, CAPRE plays a significant role in storytelling. I have shared five stories to demonstrate each part of the model. Like a carefully crafted recipe, if you take each story, you will find curiosity, appreciation, reflection, perspective and experience. The CARPE principle is there to help you build and develop your own stories. The next time you see something, demonstrate your curious side. Show your appreciation for people, situations and things and see how it adds purpose. Through reflection, build upon ideas and thoughts you have and experience the journey that results. Draw upon your perspectives and see them as unique and distinct to yourself. These will help forge the story itself. Finally, take the time to create the experience so your story is anchored. Memories are what we hold on to but it is only a memory if it is captured. The experience becomes a trigger point for your stories.

Last words for CARPE Diem

Part Two was an easy section to write because these were my stories and the concept of CARPE Diem was one that I established to help me and others come up with stories. The stories shared are 'me'. The foundation and words are the way that I lead my life and while it is not the same for all, there are some life lessons to be drawn from what has been shared.

CARPE is a concept that will enable you to take time to be curious, appreciate, reflect, provide perspective and embrace an experience. I took a simple set of footprints, applied CARPE, and built an entire workshop. What can you discover and make extraordinary out of the ordinary? Use this section as a platform to start understanding your extraordinary voice.

"You cannot open a book without learning something."
~ Confucius

~ Quick Thoughts ~

PART THREE

People who say it cannot be done should not interrupt those who are doing it.
    ~George Barnard Shaw

While Part One of this book was about the purpose of storytelling, what makes a good story, and why tell stories. Part Two showcased some examples of stories using CARPE Diem as the principle and how you can start to build your own stories. Part Three is more about you. How can you use every concept up to this point and start to incorporate and build your own personal stories.

How your life is a puzzle and stories pull it together

Personal storytelling is very much like a giant jigsaw puzzle scattered about. Think of the pieces as segments of your stories. Some of the pieces are upside down, others are clumped together. You slowly start trying to assemble and organize them and try to make sense of what you are building.

Imagine realizing that your giant jigsaw puzzle does not have a cover picture so you do not know what you are building. You have no frame of reference to pull from and only know that you need to continue pulling the pieces together. You feel anticipation and concern because you feel like you should know what it is that you are trying to solve. Does this concept of the puzzle sound familiar? Perhaps it sounds like your life or your career search?

We often go through life trying to find the answers and the image on the outside of the box. However, you do not know how to find the answers because you do know what the questions are. Sometimes we spend a lifetime trying to find the image so we decipher what this puzzle is supposed to look like. But at some point, we come to a realization that there is no cover picture. Like a puzzle, we have to build our puzzle, one story, one experience, one piece at a time. It is a realization that there are no answers to life but just more questions; however, they are the questions we need to ask ourselves.

How does this apply to storytelling? Well, your stories are the collection of images you pull together. For example, if you are taking this puzzle challenge and you start seeing a few pieces of a chimney, a door and a window. You start to think, there is a house here. Now you start to pull other pieces that might resemble a house and as you are starting to see the shape of the house. All of a sudden, you turn another piece over and you find a piece of a mast from a ship. Without hesitation, you find a porthole and part of the anchor in the scattered puzzle pieces. You realize that you are no longer building a house (which sits half finished) and you are now building a ship. Just as you pull pieces of the ship and now put those pieces together (and the house still sits unfinished), you find a part of a yellow car. The house is not done; the boat is not complete because now you shift your attention to building a car. This is how your life goes about as you build sections and try to understand what the finished image will be.

The discovery of these pieces in random fashion does not allow you to finish any one area because it prompts you to carry on with your most recent image. What you find though, as time passes by, you start seeing a pattern and areas where the boat, the house and the car start to fit in. If these are stories, they may feel random as separate life experiences, but what you need to do is see how they fit together. You cannot build a jigsaw puzzle by throwing all the pieces in the air (even if you wish you could) and having them land in a perfect fashion to form the image. The puzzle, much like your stories takes time to realize; time for the pieces to fit together.

Apply CARPE to your stories and identify how they connect together. As something happens today, think about an image or an instant in the past that happened that might relate to the present. You might not have anticipated or appreciated what that story meant at that moment in time, but after seeing a few more pieces of the puzzle, suddenly they connect together and hold more meaning.

There was a time when I was a recent university graduate and I was mopping floors and emptying garbage bins in a hospital. Although this was not my ideal position, I was not going to let it deflate or defeat me. I knew this was something I had to do and I would learn something. Only later did I realize the life lessons I learned and how much more this experience would mean to me and these lessons still sit with me today.

Years later, I found myself in a situation where I could not deal in absolutes and I needed to take a step back and appreciate things from a much deeper perspective. This is when I thought back to my time as a janitor and drew two sections of my jigsaw puzzle and it started to make sense.

This has happened multiple times in my life and I have a fairly good idea of what my life puzzle is looking like now and an idea of the broader image. Now, my challenge is to find the missing pieces. Who knows if my jigsaw puzzle will ever be finished? I am just enjoying the challenge of seeing what I can make of it and the pieces that represent stories, people, situations and objects.

Source of inspiration - memories

One does not have to look too far for inspiration to write stories. They are right around you and within you. Memories are one of the most valuable resources you can tap into for personal stories. They could be childhood experiences or something that happened the other day. Some individuals may think the experience needs to be grand to be memorable but that is not the case. Daily experiences show us where we have come from and can guide us to where we are going. Memories are a convenient way (a zip file of sorts) for our brain to help us keep our stories intact for future use. Without this zip file, our mind would be made up of jumbled thoughts and actions.

No one can better describe your memories because they are yours, you have experienced it. Often we may meet someone or visit a new place but only keeping the surface impressions of that interaction in our memory. Digging deeper and pulling out aspects has helped me better recall key points. Using different senses can help capture the memory and in the future help unlock the details. The best way to recall a memory is to create a trigger point. A trigger point is something that helps you recall a memory in a very vivid way and it can be a small aspect that you remember.

For example, I recall being 18 years old and visiting Fiji for the first time. I remember getting off the plane at 3:00AM and being hit with the intense heat and smell of sugar cane. I also recall sitting in my aunt's house at the top of a hill and closing my eyes, listening to the palm trees rustle as the wind swept through them. In the morning, the cooing doves would wake you up. To this day, the sounds and smells of that trip are my triggers and helps add further depth to that experience. When I think with these two senses, I am drawn to many more thoughts and memories that have become the foundations for additional stories.

These memories act as connecting puzzle pieces; pulling sections together to add new purpose and meaning. So you might be asking what the sugar cane, palm trees and cooing doves have to do with anything. Well, they are my memories. They are reminders of a youthful time, the people who I know, and the experiences I encountered and created many long lasting stories. The mind can be an amazing thing. I still recall that the number one song on the music charts in August 1978 was Boney M's *'Brown Girl In the Ring'*. My cousins and I listened to this tune until we wore out the record needle.

It is never too late to start building your own triggers. Think about a place you visited, someone you met, or an experience you encountered. What is the first and foremost thing you recalled about this experience? Now, start thinking about what else might be included with this experience. Build and add to the trigger. Start adding descriptors to make the puzzle more complete. Take individual pieces and start forming it into a section of your puzzle.

I will discuss the power of journaling or blogging later because it is a method to help you create purpose and meaning and help you formulate a story. What is important is that your memories are important to you and are yours alone.

Do I have what it takes?

Storytelling was not something I started to do overnight. Time and realization helped me become more reflective and understand the depth of what was happening around me. You are also never too old to become a storyteller because I never really saw myself as a writer or blogger until I was 49 years old.

While I can teach you models, tips, and tricks, to become a better storyteller, I believe it would be irresponsible not to start by looking at your mindset. Are you prepared to understand yourself better in order to start pulling stories? To ensure you can harness the full power of stories to change yourself, your relationships, and your life in dramatic and positive ways, you have to examine your behaviours and beliefs.

Most people rush into the technique of telling stories and then wonder why nothing changed – why they did not become a better storyteller. Often someone's mindset influences your success or failure in telling better stories.

I hope your goal in reading this book is not just to read the words, but rather to achieve new levels of skill and sustained behavioural change. I believe that journey starts with ensuring you have complementary beliefs that support your success. Your belief shapes and influences your behavior. You have an established foundation of history and memories that are a cache of familiarities. As you move forward, you start to draw upon these experiences.

Often times it is easy to limit our understanding of the world and our own beliefs. Similar to coming up to a fence where the view is partially obscured and you can only see part of what lies on the other side, we get frustrated that we cannot see the entire picture. It might be time for some creativity and use your other senses to help describe what you cannot see.

Children have a powerful capacity to imagine and make images come to life. As we matured, we started replacing our imagined world with the reality of what we saw and experienced. To be reflective is to blend what you can see with what you cannot see and make sense of it as a whole. Your belief is critical in this aspect. We all have our own perspective and idea of what the world holds. What one person sees might be different than what you see or understand. Simple things in life might not be obvious to you but is significant to another.

One day, I was delivering a workshop on storytelling and part of the session was to have participants think about an incident to write about. I try to prompt with thoughts like, *'Tell me about the last movie you saw?"* or, *"What was your favorite vacation memory and why"*. As people started to write, I saw one person who just sat there and was trying but could not think of anything. I went to her and kneeled down and when I asked her what was wrong, she said she could not think if anything to write about. I asked her if she had ever traveled anywhere and she said that she went to New Zealand. I asked her to tell me about what was important about her trip there. She was hesitant because she did not think it important but it was something that stuck with her. She responded, *"Being able to walk around the streets with no shoes."* My response was to ask *'Why?'* She started to explain it to me and suddenly stopped because she realized she was telling me a story. She smiled because she now understood what I was alluding to. She had found a trigger and it was about not wearing shoes in New Zealand and what that meant to her.

There were two important aspects about this example. First, this person did not think that it was important enough to tell this story. Who would care if I could wear shoes or not in New Zealand? Her belief was that it was not interesting and as such, others would not find it interesting;

however, this was a trigger and it released even more memories. It does not matter if people will resonate with the story or not. If it is important to you, you will find a way to tell an interesting story. Not everyone will be interested but some who will connect and relate to you. Remember the 15/70/15 rule; 15% will be immediately turned off and not care about going barefoot in New Zealand. Fifteen percent will completely relate to you and become engaged, perhaps because they have shared the same experience. The remaining 70% will find some purpose and significance in what you are talking about. One side of the 70% spectrum may find one key element interesting while the other extreme will gain valuable insight.

Secondly, asking 'why' was the other key ingredient to this example. By asking 'why', we start to unlock important aspects that add purpose and meaning and allows us to dig below the surface and looking past the obvious. In this case, a simple question of asking why walking around the streets of New Zealand barefoot was important. Asking 'why' of anything can be a powerful tool because we are often only thinking of experiences at the surface level. The idea is you keep going till you exhaust your 'why'. This is how you find your depth, by asking yourself 'why'. Often times I think I might know what is important but when I go on a journey to ask myself 'why', it offers different perspectives to build upon my beliefs. The road I start may not be the road I end up travelling along or end up on.

After you have asked 'why', make sure to use who, what, where, when and how to add substance and colour to your story. Not all of these questions apply but once you have the depth of 'why' the other questions help you collect the details that can help make your story more engaging for an audience.

Know yourself – discover the stories

What defines you?

At the outset of the book, we talked about putting 'you' at the centre of the story. This can be difficult if we have not taken the time to understand 'you'. Often times we are focused on the destinations and getting from here to there. You think, *"Once I graduate university, I will start my job,"* or, *"Once I get the job, I can start thinking about a Master's Degree"* and this goes on and on. We really don't focus on the journey or what makes up who we are.

To help you realize your foundation, take time to think and reflect about yourself. Consider and write down about five key words that make up who you are. I use five as the number because it provides a fairly broad perspective of who you are. You may think it is a simple exercise, but it is about taking the time to reflect and asking 'why' the words are important. It might even be an opportunity to ask someone what words they would use for you. When you have some words, the next step is to look deeper and examine the words and see how they are related to each other and does it fully explain who you are? If you build on these words, you will start to create a better grasp of what engages you and what your passions are and it will help to transform your ideas and incidents into stories.

> What are five key elements that make up who you are?

Action:

Take some time and think of 5 words to describe who you are. Ask yourself if these words are your foundation and create an idea who you are. Pick your words and then see how they are related. Go deeper and ask 'why' you these words are important to you. Ask others what they would use as words to describe you. Do those words match your words? If not, what words are further in line with you?

Write for yourself

Someone once said, *"Dance as if no one is watching."* The same rule applies to writing, so *"Write as if no one is reading."* One of the fundamental rules is to start off by writing for you. By writing your own thoughts and not having to share, you can talk about anything you want. It takes time to gain the confidence to start sharing. For many years I had my stories clutched tightly. If you are not comfortable diving into the pool, you can start by dipping your toe in. Start small but keep writing.

The blank page

How and where do I start my stories? I have a blank page of paper before me and a pen in hand, but how do I get started? I either have infinite ideas and thoughts but I can't grasp at any or I am drawing a complete blank on how to begin. You are asking me to write a story but what shall I write about? These questions can be a daunting task! We sometimes get paralyzed by the sheer request to share a story because we think it is not important, interesting or where to start? If someone asks you to share what is unique, interesting or special about you, you are not sure what to say. Will I be deemed to be bragging or it is really not interesting?

If you are staring at a blank page, not sure where to begin, don't put too much pressure on yourself. Sometimes people think that they have to put together the masterpiece right at the outset. They will put their thoughts down, edit, read, edit, read, edit, read and throw it away. The perfect piece is not something you should struggle with.

> *The blank page can be difficult...what can you do to get through this?*

Even this book is likely not perfect but I have written it with the intent to help others. With honest intensions, I can only share my experiences and learnings and hope to positively influence your ability to tell stories. There are times when I have hit roadblocks and have not been able to move forward. These are a normal part of writing.

So where to begin? It really takes just a nugget to get started with a thought that then emerges into a few words that then, put together, becomes a paragraph. This paragraph then pulls another thought and this starts supporting the first paragraph and before you know it, the page is full. The following are ways that you might be able to start putting pen to paper.

A picture speaks many words

Sometimes we are so focused on the written words that we get bogged down with language. We try to find the perfect words and descriptors; however, we also get frustrated if the way we think and the way we write are disconnected.

One way around this is to write while looking at an image. If you were to look at a piece of art or a photograph and you had to describe it to someone who could not see it, what would you write? Would you provide a broad overview and then start narrowing in on the image or would you look at specific parts and how they all fit together so it helps the recipient draw the pieces to together?

There is no right or wrong way to do this. It is more about you looking at an image and pulling thoughts forward and trying to tell the story that you see. Many times, no two people will see the image the same way or the way they would share with another person.

If you are describing the sky, tell the receiver what it looks like beyond just telling them that you see the sky. Are there clouds? Does it look like it is dawn or dusk? Is the image bright or is it subdued? Does the sky make you happy or sad? Are we getting ready for a storm or is it calm skies? As you can see, there are many ways to describe what you see.

Action:

Take a look at the images on the following pages and either write or think about what you see. Take time on each image and exhaust your thoughts before moving to the next one. A notes page is provided for each to jot down your thoughts. For each image, go beyond the obvious and add significance to it. Write about the things we might not see. Talk about the things and people who you see and who might they be? For the images with objects, what does the image do for you? What does it make you think about? If it helps, use bullets to capture key words and then add meaning to the bullets. You will find some initial thoughts for each picture but don't be limited by these.

Ilia Bykov has graciously provided three images on the following pages - http://www.iliabykov.portfoliobox.me/portrait

Sam Thiara

- *Tell me what you observe in this photo.*
- *What does the Buddha head in the roots say to you?*
- *How might the Buddha head have gotten there?*
- *What do you think about when you look at this shot?*
- *How does it make you feel?*

~ Notes ~

Ilia Bykov

- *What is behind this shot? Tell me what you think he is up to.*
- *Why this place/object/person?*
- *What is the connection between the person and the teddy bear?*
- *What do you think about when you look at this shot?*
- *Have you done something recently that was silly? Tell me about it*

~ Notes ~

Ilia Bykov

- *When you see a clock, what message does it provide you?*
- *What might you think about when you see a clock?*
- *What is behind this shot? What story might it contain?*
- *What do you think about when you look at this shot?*
- *How does it make you feel about?*
- *The clock says it is 1:37pm, what did you do yesterday at this time?*

~ Notes ~

Ilia Bykov

- What might you tell me about the image if I could not see it?
- What do you think about when you look at this shot?
- Is the person scared, playing around, or surprised? Could be
    something else?
- What emotions do you feel when you see this photo?

~ Notes ~

Sam Thiara

- Tell me what you see in this image? Describe the scene.
- Why do you think the person is standing there? What might he
be thinking?
- When you look at this image, how does it make you feel? Does
it make you feel calm, reflective or something else? Why?
- If you have been to a beach, what memory does it bring for you?

~ Notes ~

Complete the sentence

If you find that you need some writing practice, a simple exercise is to take the first few lines of a sentence and then add to it with your thoughts. It could be a simple phrase with an opportunity to add significance to it. For example, if you had the sentence: "I enjoy travelling because…" It then provides you the ability to add your perspective to this incomplete phrase. Avoid the urge to provide a simple short answer. Instead, take it as a trigger to write about why you like to travel and add in a places you have been. Don't be afraid to go in a new tangent and don't make your response abrupt. The idea is to use the incomplete sentence to start an inner conversation. Try to use descriptive words and write from a personal view.

Action:
Look at the following incomplete phrases and add your views and perspectives to make it more than complete. If you find that your response starts a new tangent, keep on going. The first question asks about your favorite movie, respond but then perhaps go into details why you like the movie, what other movies have you seen that are related that you enjoyed or did not enjoy. Why did you enjoy it over other movies?

- *My favorite movie was…because…*
- *I have a passion for…because…*
- *Yesterday, I wound up…*
- *Currently, I am doing (career) and I would like to be…because…*
- *If I could work on a community project, I would like to do…because…*
- *If money were no object, I would…because…*
- *I would like to sit and talk to…because*
- *I consider (insert name) as a leader because…*

The three minute challenge

At times, we try to think of the perfect story. We stop because we find that we are unsure of what to write. We are too concerned with the structure that we forget what the essence of what we want to share. It can be frustrating to try and put thought to paper when you are concerned with how it sounds. The initial part is to just get something down. You can revise it later but do not try to edit as you write.

A great exercise to try is to sit and write for 3 minutes straight about anything you would like but the trick is to not stop writing and to not go back and change anything. If you begin to go on a new tangent, do not stop, just keep going. It could be about your last vacation or something that happened at work.

Action:

Get a timer ready and set a timer to three minutes. Pick some random topic and just write solidly for three minutes. If you have a difficult time coming up with an idea, then pick one from below. Don't go back to change anything and just write till you exhaust the three minutes. Set the timer, head down and – GO!

Here are some ideas to get you started and to take the 3 minute challenge and fill it with thoughts and memories:

- *Recall a childhood memory where you were surprised – what was it and how did you feel?*
- *Who do you consider to be a leader and why?*
- *If you had to choose between financial wealth or meaningful change, which would you choose and why?*
- *If you could meet anyone, who would it be and what would you talk about?*
- *If you could visit any country, where would you go and why?*
- *Think about something you have seen in the news that annoyed you and is there something you can do about it?*
- *What is your greatest sports memory (either that you were part of or watched) and*
- *If you could be in any movie or TV show, which one would it be and why?*

Letter writing

For me, the foundations of storytelling and writing emerged from letter writing as I would always use letters to communicate with my grandmother in England. We would just go back and forth and find things to talk about.

A letter is a written conversation between you and the receiver. An opportunity here is for you to sit down and write someone a physical letter (not email). Write down your thoughts and then without changing anything, fold the piece of paper, put it into an envelope and seal it (so you can't go back and make changes) and make sure to mail it to them. This could be someone who you have not spoken to in a long time or someone who is near and dear that you want to just send a reminder on what they mean to you. What I appreciate about letter writing is that it is not as threatening as trying to write some thoughts on a blank piece of paper.

Action:

Find someone you have not spoken to in a while. Write them a letter and forward it to them by post. When writing the letter, don't go back and change the content. Write it, put it in an envelope and send it off! Simple as that! If you can't think of anyone, write to me!

More about your beliefs and behavior

The basis of the previous writing exercises has been about your beliefs, behaviours and perspectives. No two people would really have the same story emerge about their favorite travel destination. Sure, they might pick the same place but it might be for different reasons. For example, I visited Phuket, Thailand. For some, it is a busy and bustling destination to do as much as possible. For me, it was about being in seclusion so I could tackle this book without any imposed interruptions. I was looking for quiet and found it.

One leads to the other. Your beliefs will shape your behavior and response. Think of belief as your background and the behavior as your reactive mode to any situation that arises. Your beliefs will guide your response. For example, consider the following three examples.

- If you believe it matters to exercise, do you think you are more likely to exercise than someone who believes exercise isn't important? You bet you are!
- If you believe it matters to always drive within the speed limit, do you think you are more likely to drive within the speed limit than someone who believes it is okay to speed sometimes? You bet you are!
- If you believe taking something that is not yours is never okay, do you think you are less likely to steal than someone who believes stealing is justified in certain circumstances? You bet you are!

In any of these three examples, you will feel more at ease when your behaviours align with your beliefs. You will feel pleased that you made time to go for a run, that you obeyed all the rules of the road, and that you avoided the temptation to download a free, but illegal, copy of that new movie (or my book) you've wanted to see.

In these situations, your behaviour is in line with your beliefs. So what is the flip-side of this? Well, not surprisingly, it occurs when your actions are out of alignment with your beliefs.

In these three examples, what occurs when you don't exercise because you are busy at work, when you break the rules of the road to get to your appointment on time, when you downloaded that new movie, so you didn't have to wait for it to be available on Netflix.

> *I hope your goal is to achieve new levels of skill and sustained behaviour change.*

When there is disparity between your actions and your beliefs, you will feel uncomfortable. This internal tension makes it difficult for you to take the *action* required to become a better storyteller. You must have a personal connection to the story and if there is *misalignment*, it will be more difficult to tell or share your story. Your story emerges through you and it is only when you are authentic about the content does it flow more freely. It is a lot easier to tell a story that you align to than one that has to be fabricated.

So why would we concern ourselves with beliefs and behaviours in a book on the topic of stories? It is to ensure that you can harness the full power of stories to change yourself, your relationships, and your life in dramatic and positive ways. If you believe it, it is a lot easier to tell it and share it.

I hope your goal in reading this book is not just to read the words, but rather to achieve new levels of skill and sustained behavioural change – and I believe that starts with making sure you have beliefs in place to support your success.

Does Telling a Good Story Matter?

Essentially, I'm asking you if you *care* about being able to tell a good story. Think about the motivational power of caring about something; truly, deeply, caring about something.

What are some examples of deep caring?
- A mother for the safety of her children.
- An Olympic athlete for winning her competition.
- An entrepreneur for growing his business.

In each of these instances, how driven is the mother, the athlete, or the entrepreneur to go to extreme lengths? You can likely think of times when you have seen them take massive action and endure great sacrifices to accomplish their goals. They did this because they *care*.

It is my fundamental belief that without the proper degree of motivation, you will struggle and encounter tremendous challenges to becoming a better storyteller.

Why do I believe so strongly that this is true? In order to get better at anything, storytelling included, you need to be motivated to direct and sustain the level of effort required to learn and improve. This does not just apply to storytelling but also to life experiences and goals. The following is what I have encountered in life that has helped me to grow and shape as an individual.

> *Motivation is the processes that account for an individual's intensity, direction, and persistence of effort toward achieving a goal.*

- You will need to dedicate time that could be spent elsewhere.
- You will need to forego doing easier more familiar things.
- You will need to step outside of your comfort zone.
- You will need to push through fear, doubt, and uncertainty.
- You will need to avoid distractions.
- You will need to learn through reading, watching, and listening.
- You will need to practice through creating, writing, and speaking.

Action:
Take some time to answer the following questions that help build off your foundation on caring using the points above to help guide you.

- *Tell me, 'why' do you care about being able to tell a good story?*
- *If you could tell better stories, how might this help you in your journey*
- *What might change in your life if you could tell better stories*

Are you convinced it matters? Dig deep down inside and truly explore the reason you bothered to pick up and read this book. Were you curious about 'story telling'? Or did you really want to use this book to become a better storyteller? Did you want to be able to do something that you were not previously able to do?

A Base to Work From – Our Own Expertise

You already know a lot about what makes for a good story – right? You should. You consume stories all the time in the form of books, plays, movies, TV shows, listening to friends, hearing speeches.

Stories are around us, all the time. What you probably don't notice is why you enjoy some stories more than others. Personal preference certainly plays a role, just as it does in musical tastes. Some people like Rock and some people like Classical. However, across all good stories and all good music, you will find patterns; characteristics that are common to any good story and any good music.

Sometimes it is relatedness. You can appreciate something more because you have experienced it or you understand how it feels. Climbing Mount Everest might not be reasonable for me. I have read stories about it, watched documentaries, know mountain climbers, but I can only base it on my perceptions of what I have observed or read. I have some related concepts but until I climb Mount Everest, I can only imagine what it might be like. To be in a situation allows one the privilege to tell compelling stories because they have the credibility to share from their experiences.

This does not mean that we all have to go and climb Everest to understand mountaineering but there are those with more credibility to tell the story better than others. Saying that, there is a connectedness we share. As mentioned, I will not be climbing Mount Everest; however, I have read a couple of interesting true accounts of the ascent and decent of Everest. In this situation, I would not act as the expert but rather as a participant in a conversation because of what I have read. I am comfortable being an expert in other areas like leadership, student engagement or storytelling. What one needs to do is find their niche, experiences or happenings and use that as a base. Sometimes these will be able to provide a more general scope so that you can have a larger platform to build and express your stories. It is okay to be a storyteller at times and a participant at other times.

Action:

Take a moment to consider what you already knew, prior to picking up this book, about what makes for a good story and a good storyteller.

A good story has…

1. _____
2. _____
3. _____
4. _____
5. _____

A good storyteller can…

1. _____
2. _____
3. _____
4. _____
5. _____

Now, take a look at the lists you have created. Put a checkmark next to any item that also aligns to what you have learned through reading this book.

You can probably see that you are already creating links between your personal knowledge and your new knowledge on this subject. This integration into your existing ways of thinking about stories is an important step towards developing into a better storyteller.

Consider the lists above and how frequently and effectively you exemplify these traits in your stories and in yourself. If it's "all the time" or "often" that's great! If it's "never" or "rarely" that's okay too – the point here is to establish an understanding of where you are currently. We start where you are at and build from there.

Next Steps – What Have You Learned?

While you already know a lot about what makes a good story and a good storyteller, we hope that you have learned something from this book. Which few nuggets of wisdom really stood out and caught your attention? Which ideas surprised you? What did you find most interesting? What was most relevant to you personally?

Take a moment to jot down five of your key nuggets so far.

Action:

I have learned...

    1. _____

    2. _____

    3. _____

    4. _____

    5. _____

That's great! I'm hoping your list was easy to create, due to an avalanche of excellent thoughts coming to mind for you right away. Now that you have an idea of what you learned, how about taking each of them further to then see how you work to build on your personal development on storytelling.

Who?

Two fundamental tenets of effective storytelling are to know your audience and know your purpose. This means knowing who you are trying to communicate with and why you are trying to communicate with them.

> *Stories are a way to define ourselves - our identity and position in the world - to ourselves and others.*

When it comes to storytelling, you will find that many of the books on the subject focus on the audience being "others". However, a subset of these books focus on the stories we tell ourselves. Just think about this for a moment. If our own stories can shape the beliefs and behaviours of others, sometimes even complete strangers, imagine how powerfully these stories shape us.

When we tell a personal story several times it becomes engrained in us. It becomes the 'E' – Experience in CARPE. In a personal story, we always have a role, usually the protagonist or an observer. The way we describe making decisions, forming our opinions and emotional feelings we relay to our audience/reader; these are all descriptive of our own personal experiences. It is the culmination of these experiences that make us who we are. They shape us into ourselves and create our identity.

When we tell a powerful story about a "defining moment" in our lives, the impact the story has on our sense of identity is even stronger. A defining moment can be described as a situation when something significant happened to you or when you made a significant decision. In either case, in a defining moment story, you will notice that the story holds special meaning for you. It describes an event that dramatically shaped you, your relationships, or another important aspect of your life.

Notice that any time you tell someone a story, you are telling it to yourself as well. You are "listening in" on the story too. Consider this example. Think about what happens when you tell a friend about a movie you recently saw. As you describe the characters, the setting, the plot, you are seeing parts of the movie play again in your head. It's like you are watching the movie a second time, as you listen in on your description of it.

Action:
Try this exercise with a partner. Sit back to back with one person watching the TV or computer screen and play a Mr. Bean episode. The reason for Mr. Bean is that it is 99% visual. Then at the end, describe what you saw to the person with their back to the screen. You can even stop half way and switch roles.

Even as you do your best to provide an accurate summary of the movie to your friend, some parts of the movie may become distorted. Things may be forgotten, exaggerated, and/or misplaced. The distortion is caused by many effects, not the least of which is the addition of your opinions about the movie. Your *summary* is really a *review*.

As has been reinforced throughout this book, whether we are aware of it or not, we constantly interpret and evaluate our lived experiences. And if our *stories* are merely a revisiting of our own lived experiences, shouldn't we expect that we would constantly interpret our stories as well?

> *You are already telling a story, so why not make it a good one?*

I believe that the stories we tell can *help* or *hurt* us. If our interpretation of our stories often places us in a role of the "damsel in distress", we are more likely to make future decisions that we would expect a helpless damsel in distress to make. This is because we identify with the role we play in our stories. The more we tell those same stories – sometimes for years – the more we solidify our identity as the person we portray in our stories.

Once I had a student come into my office and we had a thoughtful discussion. One thing I noticed is that while he was speaking, he kept saying, *"The problem with this situation is…."* And then he would continue with, *"I found this was a problem when I tried…"* He kept using the word 'problem' in his conversation with me. I had to stop him and ask him to replace the word problem with the word opportunity. By saying problem, he was only focusing on the limitations. By using the word opportunity, he still had the same problem, but now he was seeking a solution. Change a word, change your life. This is just one way where we can try to shift a word to try and change the context of the story.

Now, while there is a dark side where stories may hurt us, this also presents an opportunity. If we want to use stories to help us, we can craft stories that are empowering. These are stories that put us in charge of ourselves, our relationships, and the quality of our lives overall. Stories highlight the power we have to make choices that will lead to the things we want in our lives. Stories can also focus on the good, rather than the bad; take the optimist's "glass half full" perspective, rather than dwelling in a place of pessimism. For example, earlier I shared about my father being a paraplegic and how our family was impacted by the accident of February 10, 1972. Instead of dwelling on it as a negative, we framed it into another perspective that has made our lives richer.

More About the YOU Versus Others

We sometimes get focused on what other people are doing or saying and start comparing ourselves to others. We ask ourselves, *"What would so and so do in this instance"*, if you are thinking about a story? If I am talking about a particular subject, how might someone react or care about what I am saying?

I think it is important to start focusing on **you** and the stories you hold. You are telling stories but you might not be fully aware of it. Think back or start looking at what you say and how you share, are there stories embedded in your conversations? If so, what do you usually share with other people?

Action:
Answer the following question - I often tell a story about…

- _____
- _____
- _____
- _____
- _____

Why do you tell these particular stories most often, of all the stories you could tell?

~ Quick Thoughts ~

What is the motivation to tell these stories? How are they serving you? Do they make you feel happy? Do they make people laugh? Do they garner you sympathy?

What I am trying to uncover here are your *motivations*. The reasons you chose to tell these particular stories.

> Stories of the past (yesterday) inform how we behave now (today) and in the future (tomorrow).

Understanding your motivations will help you consciously decide what story to tell and when to tell it. This will help you better understand the purpose for telling the story. How are these stories helping or hurting you? How are these stories helping or hurting others?

Your story can have an *impact*. Sometimes that impact may be putting someone to sleep, but there will always be an impact. If someone does fall asleep when you are telling a story (let's assume it is not a bedtime story), this signals a disconnect between your *intent* and your *impact*. Intent is what you set out to do and the impact is the result. Let's explore this concept of intended purpose and perceived impact further by asking a question.

Why?

People don't care about what you do. They care about why you do it. The underlying "so what?" of your story is what matters. Why are you telling this story? What is the purpose?

Anytime we communicate with someone else, we are trying to impact people's thoughts, feelings, and actions. All of our communication has intended and inferred meaning. Intended meaning comes from the sender and inferred meaning is perceived by the receiver.

However, there are many challenges that distort the communication process. We often call this gap the *difference between intent and impact*. Take for example, when you talk to voice dictation software, such as Siri on the iPhone, and how it often does not correctly translate your spoken words into text. What you intended to say and the actual outcome was different.

Looking For Prompts and Signals

We need to be aware of and consider the world around us. Surface imagery would be the first thing we observe or see. Typical responses would be quite short or abrupt. Have you ever noticed in your daily interactions when you ask others how they are, the common response is "good" or "busy" with no additional context. It is almost a set response to a set question.

To help you become a better storyteller, try adding depth to your daily conversations. Try to avoid the immediate reactive response but take some time to provide a more detail. Detailed responses will help you add and build imagery and ease your transition to better storyteller.

Rainy days are not the only times that I can sit back with a cup of hot tea and reflect on my actions and take time to appreciate the world around me. You do not need to use a lot of descriptive worlds about rain to add meaning, but you can use other context to convey what rain means to me.

Other People's Stories

One of the easiest ways to become a better storyteller is to listen to lots of stories. A writer may read a lot of literature and a movie producer may watch a number of films, but these activities will not automatically make them better writers or producers. One could theorize it would improve their pop culture trivia skills instead.

What needs to be added to reading, watching, or listening is the specific act of observation. Rather than passive consumption, it is about active engagement. A concept I often share is to both listen and observe. Merely hearing someone speak is a surface observation, but to listen and observe, you have taken it to a deeper level of understanding.

Action:

Ask at least three other people, "so what's your story?" It might be better to put some context here rather than just going up to someone and asking them the question. Try to look for an organic response. As they tell you, perhaps go back and ask them to expand on a particular section. If this sounds awkward, you can ask someone the following way:

- *I am looking to tell stories better. Could you please help me by telling me more about you? What have you done that you enjoy and why? Who do you respect and admire and why? What childhood memories do you hold dear?*

When they tell you their story, listen for any or all of the following:

- **Characters** – What do their characters tell you about the storyteller?
- **Purpose** – Why are they telling this story? What do they want you to think, feel, or do?
- **Scene, setting, or situation** – What senses are they using to describe? What visual imagery are they portraying?
- **Challenge, task, or obstacle** – Why was the issue a difficult? What problems did it pose?
- **Action or solution** – What actions did the storyteller or other characters? Was action a potential solution?
- **Climax or punch line** – What made the climax the high point of the story?
- **Result or conclusion** – What was the resolution? Was there resolution?
- **Moral (if specifically stated or one you interpret)** – What does it mean to you? What does it say about life? What is the lesson to be learned?

Your Journey Forward

We haven't tried to tackle everything related to storytelling in this book, so clearly there will be some areas where you may still be curious.

Given that Personal Storytelling is not all encompassing and the fact that there is always more to learn on any topic, what else would you like to learn about storytelling and why?

Action:

I would like to learn…

1. _____,

    because _____

    _____

2. _____,

    because _____

    _____

3. _____,

    because _____

    _____

While understanding *what* you want to learn and *why* is a great start, you will need to take some kind of action in order to actually learn. As you know, when actions are specific and time-bound they are more likely to happen. What specific steps will you take and by when, to learn more about storytelling?

Action:
I will...

1. _____

   _____

   by _____

2. _____

   _____

   by _____

3. _____

   _____

   by _____

Sharing your stories

A story can only become significant to the extent it is shared with others. As a storyteller, you will have to decide how widely you would like to share your story. A story can be personal and strictly for you alone, it can be shared with a few close friends, or it can be something you want to share with the world.

Once you document your thoughts, it is entirely up to you how broadly you distribute it. A journal may be a good tool for personal stories. You can use personal journal entries to help you build the foundation of a story for a wider audience. There are also more public forums for you to use if you wish to incorporate storytelling in your daily life and share with the public.

The following are some ways you can get your message across.
- Journaling
- Letter writing
- Blogging
- Social media
- Public speaking

Journaling – Whether you decide to write for yourself or for others, journaling is probably one of the most critical pieces to help you forge your stories. Journaling is the process of capturing your thoughts in a raw format. You can always go back and modify your writing; however, journaling is where you write your thoughts down based on what and how you are feeling in the moment. What I appreciate most about journaling is how it can help capture the 'organic' you. It can be as simple as using pen and notebook or documenting it electronically in a Word document and formally editing it into an elegant piece.

Journaling helps you to understand 'you'. The process of journaling allows you to make sense of your thoughts and create a better appreciation of who you are. It allows you to take a break from the everyday to reflect and write down your thoughts. You can set a process in place, such as to write in your journal at the end of the day, or when things come to mind. The thoughts can be recorded as one time entries that are never looked at again or they can be part of general themes and concepts for a larger written piece like a blog. Once you have written a few journal entries, you can review past entries to help you make sense of what happened and how you felt at that moment. If you are happy, write about it and try to understand why. If you are sad and write about it, ask why? Asking yourself these questions will help you create greater understanding of who you are and what emotions you are feeling. This is the foundation for self-reflection.

At the outset of this section, I spoke about how our stories are pieces of a jigsaw puzzle. Journaling allows you to take the time to realize how they fit together. By documenting your words and thoughts, you capture them for the future and it helps to make sense of 'you'.

Letter writing – I referenced letter writing as a technique to storytelling. There is comfort in writing a letter. It is an action that allows you to put your thoughts on paper rather than electronic format. You have to describe everything; the situation, person and place to the other person in detail. You are only able to use verbal language to communicate with the recipient. You are creating the images for the recipient.

You can send a letter to someone you know or you can write a letter and mail it to yourself. The act of letter writing is what is most important. You do not have to spend a lot of time thinking about how you want to say things; just write to the other person. I am sure that they are more interested in hearing from you.

Blogging – There are many Internet blogs out there and the degree you use blogging will depend on who your audience is. If the content is just for you, then blogging can be a virtual journal. However, be aware you may inadvertently be inviting outsiders into your thoughts. With search engines and public Internet domains, someone could come across your blog. If your objective is outreach to a wider audience, blogging can be a positive tool. To engage the Internet audience, you may need to incorporate other social media tools to supplement your writing.

An example of how powerful blogging can be, in my first attempt at blogging I wrote 109 blog posts (http://sams50-50.com/) as part of my yearlong fiftieth birthday celebration. Reader traffic was guided through social media and a number of people who commented and became a part of or catalysts for future thoughts and stories I shared. Fast forward a few years, I now have a new website and blog at http://www.sam-thiara.com/ and have returned to writing. I am again using social media to guide my blog.

What is important though is that you have to have a purpose and message to convey to your audience. In my case, I provide life lessons and insights to help others. The blog has to be aligned to the writer or it will not be seen as authentic. Choose a topic and purpose that you are passionate about, journal and then start forming a story. I have had to consistently come up with new content. If you don't, you will lose your followers. This becomes a challenge for many bloggers who stop blogging and their audience base dries up. If you can't come up with your original content, then speak about or provide commentary on other articles and sources.

Writing and sharing your stories – There are a number of sites on the internet that allow one to share stories. The medium is set up that you can upload your short story, ideas and poems to a community that range in amateur authors to established pieces. All you need to do is google – 'writing and sharing your stories' and you will be amazed at the various sites available for you to explore. Depending on the site, you don't need to provide a literary masterpiece but rather your thoughts and the audience will be attracted based on your topic and writing. This becomes the first step to publicly share your stories.

Social Media – You might be surprised to know that you are probably already telling and writing stories through social media. By using Facebook, Twitter or other means, you are describing yourself and your day to the world. Sometimes the posts or tweets are rather short but in your mind are the expanded versions. Take some time to consider what you are writing while using social media and see if you can add further depth.

If you think about it, Facebook is a mechanism where you tell your friends how you are feeling or what you are doing. Take the post next time and expand upon it using descriptors (but not while on Facebook) and see if you can add purpose and further meaning.

Public Speaking – This is not something everyone is comfortable with; however, it is a powerful mechanism if you possess or build the courage for it.

Audiences look for the opportunity to hear compelling speakers share stories. These stories are often personal reflections that are related to the topic of the presentation, seminar, or conference. I often am asked how I write and present speeches, topics and stories. The process I use is determining my audience and what they want and tailoring my talk towards that; adding stories to support the message. Using CARPE, I consider what the theme is and then pull my stories from the virtual shelf as they apply. Do not panic if you do not have a lot of stories at this point. The more you reflect on your life and past, you will find several stories from memories of the life you have already lived. If not, make sure you start capturing your experiences moving forward and catalogue them for future stories.

When I am asked to help and guide people in delivery of their talks, I often tell them that there are some basic considerations.
1) If you had to talk to a group of people, what are the 3-4 key messages you would share with them? You may have many stories or thoughts but limit it to 3-4. Resist the urge to share as much as you can in the allotted time.
2) Decide why you want to share certain stories. Are they relevant to the broader presentation topic or do they just sound good?
3) If you need to, use PowerPoint images or a physical object to support your presentation. A visual can help the audience better understand, appreciate and relate to your story. For example, when I speak to university students about their personal journey, I always show them the rejection letters I received while I was searching for employment. The large pile of letters serves as strong visual to the rejection and struggle I faced.

Some final thoughts about your story building

This section was focused on assisting you with your story building through self-reflection. This included how to understand yourself so that you can apply that to your stories for authenticity and how make sense of your beliefs and perspectives. It was to help bridge my thoughts with yours.

Later we examined methods to build your stories with the use of different challenges and exercises. We also discussed options to help you get started.

Part Three is not something that you can undertake on its own and result in an instant transformation into a dynamic and engaging storyteller. Transformation takes time, but if you follow some of the guidelines discussed, it may help you to start being a storyteller or a better storyteller. This section was not about rules for storytelling and story development but rather guidelines and thoughts to help you pull in what is important to you.

PART FOUR

"The stranger who tells our stories when we cannot speak not only awakens our spirits and hearts but also shows our humanity - which others want to forget - and in doing so becomes family."
— *Mende Proverb, Sierra Leone*

We have discussed why someone might tell stories and the importance of storytelling. We have shared stories related to the CARPE principle to demonstrate the process of storytelling. Part Three provided some insight and suggested tools on how someone can build their own stories. Now it is your turn to start telling and sharing your own stories.

Each of you will have different perspectives and meanings for the stories shared so far and the ones shared below. Section Four is a series of stories and blog posts to reflect on. At the end of each of the posts, there will be a thought and a question posed to allow you to reflect and pull purpose, meaning. Take time to write down your thoughts. Some stories may have more impact than others. Some stories might not have any effect on you at all. As you will see, stories are personal. For more posts, please visit http://sam-thiara.com

I would suggest reading the posts one at a time and see the question provided at the end. Take time to think about what is being asked and then write down your thoughts. Do not try to write a literary masterpiece, focus on releasing the mind. Do not spend time thinking about grammar or spelling, the idea is to just write based on the thoughts that emerge. What does it make you think of?

Let us begin:

~ Not comfortable with comfort and uncertain about uncertainty ~

It is interesting how a word that is meant to provide us with 'comfort' can also have a double meaning. Comfort can be positive when we think about having a comfortable life; carefree, easygoing, enjoyable and stable. The word itself makes our shoulders drop and we let out a sigh. It is what we strive towards and want to be as our destination. We ask ourselves, I will be comfortable when I get that first job where I feel established. I will be comfortable when I find and settle down with my life partner. I will be comfortable when I am able to pay off the mortgage. These are all things that people will journey towards and look forward to.

On the other hand, comfort can also be seen from a negative context; it could describe a situation where we stop growing or take risks because we are too comfortable. We are afraid to rock the boat for fear of losing our comfort and we start to forget about the dreams and aspirations we had. Before you know it, you are years into a position and feeling bound because comfort has settled in and you now have lost your edge to change. We say to our self, I will just sit on the sidelines till it is time for me to retire. I retire, then what?

It is interesting that the word 'uncertainty' which is the opposite of comfort also has a double meaning. Many people fear uncertainty and ambiguity. People may like situations that are clear and obvious because it is familiar and comfortable. Uncertainty means the unknown; potentially having to change and follow a path that involves ambiguity. We are unsure of what might happen and we focus on the limitations and challenges instead of the possibilities and opportunities. It is about walking to the edge of darkness and taking a step without knowing what is going to happen.

Uncertainty also provides us that little bit of nervousness that gets us excited about the unknown and gives us the opportunity to be creative and innovative with our approach. With self-confidence and belief in your capabilities, you can make the most of challenging situations. I know individuals who have given up comfort, uprooted themselves and fundamentally changed their lives. In some cases this was to travel the world and challenge themselves or they have left a stable position to embark on a new journey of entrepreneurship. The funny part is that they always land on their feet. When you go down this path, you are not alone. There are champions and enablers who will be along your journey to help you be successful.

Ask yourself about comfort and uncertainty. Are you happy with your present situation? Is there a way to create or add uncertainty to fuel change? We must continue to grow as individuals or possibly be destined for regrets. I am not asking you to give up your comforts but to instill a bit of uncertainty. Start with small things that you can or should do and see what it leads to. You will be amazed with the outcomes. Have faith in yourself. You have much to offer and sometimes we just need to get a glimpse of what we are capable of. William G.T. Shedd said, *"A mighty ship can sit safely in a harbour; however, that is not what they were built for."* Release the lines and set the sails for the horizon.

Understand that if you have comfort, you may lack uncertainty and if you embrace uncertainty, you cannot really reside in true comfort. My choice is to set the path for uncertainty and continue to have adventures.

Thought: *We strive to comfort but is comfort a good thing? Uncertainty is also a word that we might not be comfortable with; however, we can thrive in uncertainty if we control it.*

Question: *Are you someone that strives to comfort or uncertainty? Explain which one and why. Provide an example?*

~ Your Reflections ~

~ Searching for happiness? Found it! ~

Are you a happy person? Do you really enjoy, appreciate and make the most of life so you are happy? When something goes wrong, how do you handle it? Do you let the situation dictate how you recover or do you confront the situation head on? How do you react or overcome adversity? These are all questions from the movie 'Happy' that tried to define happiness. The movie started with how we have taken so much time to understand, assess and measure depression but asked if we have taken sufficient time to do the same with happiness. When we are not in a good space, we feel things are terribly wrong and try to correct it right away without spending the time to understand the full picture. People need to take the time to understand their personal happiness.

We can do this by appreciating the small things in our life and looking at things with an open mind. Sounds a lot like the 'The Extraordinary in the ordinary.' Incorporate flow into your life and do what you want to do without feeling like it is a taxing activity. We get bogged down and caught up in our daily activities that we forget to have fun. As we age, we may feel that time is passing quickly and the opportunities to accomplish things we wanted to do are slowly slipping away. As I get older, I learn and do more.

Happy people do encounter adversity but they seem to recover quicker by allowing the situation guide their reaction. Just switching your focus from what you do not have to what you do have can impact your happiness. You can either think of your life as concentrated flavorful orange juice or watered down Kool-Aid.

What makes me happy? For me it is about gratitude, being authentic, taking the time to talk to people, being thankful for what I have, and knowing that I am on a journey. Happiness is about being present and helping others to be happy.

How about you? Are you happy? What makes you happy? If you are happy, what is it that puts a smile on your face? If you are not happy, how can WE change that?

Making others feel happy will positively impact your happiness. With a bit of light laughter, happiness can be contagious. Can you think about a time where everyone else was super happy, laughing and having a good time and you were very unhappy?

Thought: *Are you a happy person? Are you living a life that you consider to be happy?*

Question: *Think about this post for a moment and express some of the things that makes you smile or make you feel happy?*

~ Your Reflections ~

_____

_____

_____

_____

_____

_____

_____

_____

_____

_____

_____

_____

_____

_____

_____

_____

_____

_____

_____

_____

~ Taking baby steps ~

What happened from the time we learned to take our first footsteps until we were able to start walking and never had to look back? Think about the risks we took and the times we had our setbacks in those first few steps.

As a baby, we were determined by some unknown force to learn to walk and did not give up till it was done. We did not just start walking right away. It was a gradual progression from kicking legs to crawling, crawling to standing upright, holding a table for support and then letting go to take risky first step. We all fell down a lot! Children just keep trying until they are successful. I have seen this happen with my own two children and now I am chasing my little guy everywhere!

As we age, we get used to walking but something else happens, we slowly lose the openness to taking risks. Fast forward to the present and we now work in a company, settled into habits, routines and we no longer take risks. I am not talking about dangerous or irrational risks but rather those small risks that put that nervousness feeling in the pit of our stomachs.

We still have opportunities to step up and do things to challenge us but do not seem to take them. Perhaps we had a negative experience previously or it seems like too much trouble. For example, I completed my first public speaking engagement twenty years ago and I did very poorly. At that time, I had a choice to give up and never do it again because I did not do well or I could tell myself it could not be worse, so it has to be better next time. I did try again and with time and practice I slowly got better and better at it. I did not give up, kept pushing myself and was rewarded with the opportunity to present a TEDxSFU talk in 2011. This made me feel like an accomplished speaker. I am a risk taker but not a daredevil. I kept learning to walk till I got to running one step at a time

I sometimes ask myself why I take on risks. I guess it is because I will continue to challenge, grow and learn from my experiences.

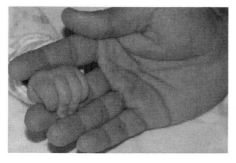

Imagine if as babies we tried to walk; we let go of the table, took a step and fell down. Then we rub our bottom and tell ourselves, *"I tried walking, that hurt too much so I am going to crawl the rest of our life."* We exhibit this behaviour with our careers, we forget to take risks even if they mean we could walk instead of crawl. We stop trying to walk. Ask yourself, when was the last time you took a risk? When did you challenge yourself within the environment you are in or to look to try something new? Let go of the table and start taking those first few steps again. I can guarantee you will fall down but you will also keep getting up and keep trying.

Thought: *As children, we take risks and learn from those experiences and keep going till we accomplish what we set out to do.*

Question: *What is the last risk you took and what was the outcome. If you have not taken a risk, why is that?*

~ Your Reflections ~

_____

_____

_____

_____

_____

_____

_____

_____

_____

_____

_____

_____

_____

_____

_____

_____

_____

_____

~ Pyar – a word to embrace ~

When I am in a reflective state or observing things, the universe starts pulling connections together and all the different pieces seem to fit. A thought comes to me like a lightning bolt and my eyes open wide with excitement. My mind tends to go on an unexplained journey every night while I sleep and provides me with a word or thought early the next morning. This post was no different and it brought me a word to share. The word is pyar. It is pronounced 'pi-yaar' and is a word in the Hindi language. The word itself is a  beautiful word. It means love. There are also different types of pyar but the type I am talking about is the rich feeling you get when you are in someone's company and you feel a strong bond or connection. It allows me to share my time with them because they matter to me.

Pyar is difficult to translate, but I will try to describe its essence. I have pyar for many people. The pyar I feel and sense I have for my students and alumni is pyar in the form of genuine respect and appreciation. It is also foundational in all the strong relationships that I establish. It is a feeling that comes from the heart. There is no better way to describe this word than the feeling you get when you sit with someone and share and you are consumed by a spiritual sense and you know this person is someone that is on your journey and you will always make time for them. While this might be for one person, it is replicated thousands of times for me. I have felt so much pyar and given so much pyar over my lifetime.

It is too bad that there is not a universal language that defines pyar so everyone would understand it. Likely a universal feeling but defined by people in different languages. 'Pyar' is the love and respect for you that comes from my heart. It is what prompts us to naturally hug when we see each other or say goodbye because a handshake will just not do. It is what will make us misty eyed when we talk. The word is a good one because I pyar you.

Thought: *Pyar is a word that means a deep appreciation in Hindi. It is a lovely sentiment and word.*

Question: *Is there someone you 'pyar'? Who is this person and why. What do they do that makes you feel this way?*

~ Your Reflections ~

~ Miles of smiles bring us together ~

Reflecting on people, have you ever wondered why are we divided by geography, race, religion, social, political or ideological differences? Who decided that the world must be divided by these differences? We have spent considerable time separating ourselves from those who are different, creating a fearful and uncertain environment. At times, we seem to be drifting farther away from one another.

We need to take the time to understand those who are different from ourselves. I have done this by visiting a number of different places, talking to others and seeing what their lives are like. Through this, you come to appreciate what life is all about.

You can learn much about others and yourself if you travel with an open mind. Your goal is not to compare who you are or what you have but rather see how we all fit together.

You also learn that we are not much different from each other; it is amazing what a smile can do to break down barriers. It is through traveling that you can start to purge those fears of others that society has instilled. Fear of the unknown and different creates an "us versus them" mentality that prevents people from really connecting or understanding on another Working with students and alumni from a variety of different backgrounds has enriched me as an individual. Although each of my students are unique; they still possess some striking similarities.

It is interesting how perceptions shape our views of people and society. When I tell people that I have had the opportunity to travel to the Middle East four separate times; I am often asked if I was ever scared of a terrorist attack or why do I put myself into a dangerous situation. The Middle East

is indeed very dangerous, perhaps not the way you might think it. I am not sure why the first question is one of safety from terrorism as I felt very safe walking the streets of Bahrain, Kuwait or Doha at midnight. The most dangerous part was that these cities lacked proper road safety and you just had to be careful to look both ways before you stepped off the curb.

Have you ever wondered why religion or politics separate us? We align ourselves to certain beliefs and ideologies and harm one another in the name of religion or politics. If we had to separate ourselves in some fashion, why not base it on blood type. Physically, blood type is more constant than any belief or ideology and if we harm each other, you would have the right blood type right next to you.

People! We are all more similar than we think. We all smile, cry, laugh and feel emotions. We all have families and friends. We all possess the need to help each other and use our eyes to see one another. We all have someone who cares about us and we all care about someone. I have always found that a smile or hug is a great tool to remove fear and to establish a solid relationship.

Thought: *We are all different; however, we also embody similarities. The world has its problems but we need to consider people from the richness of their uniqueness.*

Question: *Do you have a perception regarding a group of people? How did you come to this understanding and is it one of tolerance or intolerance?*

~ Your Reflections ~

~ Yes/No – maybe so?! ~

One challenge I have always encountered are the many requests to be a mentor, attend an event, grab a coffee to talk about life or volunteer to support an event. I never like to say no to an opportunity to help; however, the requests sometimes come in waves and the commitments can seem overwhelming. It is actually a great place to be where you feel needed and I would not have it any other way. I am sure you have had to be in a situation where you had to choose if you could be involved or not.

What I realized was that I was framing the opportunity the wrong way. Why do we often look at a situation as a 'yes/no' decision? It is easy and convenient to open up our calendar and see what our schedule looks like and respond with, "*Yes, that can fit into my schedule*" or, "*Sorry, but I have commitments and it is not going to work.*"

Instead of looking at things as 'yes/no' how about you take control and respond back with 'Here is what I can do'. It might still be a challenge but by framing it this way, you take hold of the situation.

Let me share an example. I will get requests from a student to meet up for tea (I don't drink coffee). What I do is say is that this week might be difficult, how about you provide me 2-3 dates/times next two weeks that work for you? What I have now done was to move the request to what I might be able to do as opposed to flatly saying 'no'. Do you realize that by doing this, in over 18 years, I have never turned anyone away and we are talking about hundreds of meet ups. Sometimes if you are not able to help, you can become creative - perhaps you know someone who can, you have still helped because it is 'what you can do'.

The next time someone has a request, look for the opportunity to own it. Sometimes it might not be possible and that is totally fine but see about what you can do. Be more creative than 'no'. What I have realized is that this has been one of the foundations of my success and here is 'what I will do' – share with you so you too can be successful.

Thought: *We sometimes feel like we have to deal in absolutes of yes or no but never take a moment to put ourselves in the situation where we can make a better decision*

Question: *Think back to a time where you had to decide on what you could or could not do and how did you handle that? Based on this post, how can you re-frame your response so you are not dealing in absolutes?*

~ Your Reflections ~

~ Journey or final destination – your choice? ~

Why do we anxiously rush ahead in life; trying to get to where we think we should be in only to find that upon arrival, we are off chasing the next milestone? We seem to always be striving towards that job, that promotion, that car, that perfect relationship. Then we look around at others and either feel we need what they have or because they are more accomplished, we are dejected and unaccomplished. There is so much noise and distraction around us that drives us into frenzy. We forget to have fun!

When was the last time you sat down and thought about life? – your life! I mean slowing down your pace (sleeping does not count) and appreciating what you have, reflecting on individuals and situations around you. We are so caught up in a race and trying to get from point A to B that as we near B, we are already thinking about C and D! Understand, it is not about A, B, C or D but rather the journey to get to those points that matter most. We should be focused on the journey and take the time to appreciate what we experience. It is the journey and not the final destination that should matter.

One of my favorite sayings captures this beautifully. It is called *The Station* and it is by Robert Hastings. I think you need to take a moment to read it

and realize that it captures the essence of what we need and should be doing.

Please join me on the journey; let us sit, have some tea and talk. Let us surrender to the quietness around us and clear our mind of the clutter. Sit still for a moment and reflect on who you really are and what amazing things you have accomplished. The reality is that we focus on what we do not have or who we have not become and forget about what we have and who we are. Look out the window and appreciate the scene but also see the reflection in the window that is you. We look out but sometimes see past our immediate reflection. I see the richness in the person that they sometimes do not see in themselves. Remember, the most important part of life is not the final destination but rather the journey.

Thought: *We are always focused on the final destination over the journey. The journey is the most important part as we consider the people we meet, the situations we encounter and the things we do.*

Question: *What makes up your journey? What are some of the accomplishments you have encountered that you are proud of and what lies ahead for you?*

~ Your Reflections ~

_____

_____

_____

_____

_____

_____

_____

_____

_____

_____

_____

_____

_____

_____

_____

_____

_____

_____

_____

_____

_____

_____

_____

~ Artifacts – tell-tale signs ~

Do you possess or hold something that offers you comfort and meaning? I teach an introductory course in organizational behaviour and the last lecture for the class was about organizational culture. Organizations have visible artifacts. All you have to do is to walk into a store, coffee shop, bank or business and you see visible signs that define that company. In my class, I asked what people recognize about the difference between Air Canada and WestJet. Both companies are Canadian airlines; however they are very different. Most people in class could not really think what set them apart because they never really noticed more than the difference in ticket prices. Both of these airlines are quite different in how they are organized and operated. Next time when you walk into a business, take a moment to just look around. What colours do they have? What are some of the defining ways they have designed the space? What about the people working there, how are they dressed? What does this say about the organization?

Now that we have focused on the organization, how about you? Artifacts hold your personal story. What artifacts define you?

For me, the alumni pin that I wear from Simon Fraser University is an artifact. During my first role post-graduation as a janitor, my alumni pin was tucked away, but still a symbol and reminder of my academic roots.

Years later when I returned to SFU, it became a reminder of my goal to help students be able to have a better experience that I. There are many artifacts that I hold on to that define who I am.

What things can you think of that holds purpose and meaning for you? There are things that you have had given to you or that you have found and attach a memory to it that captures its importance. There are likely many artifacts around that just need to be recognized.

When was the last time you gave someone something that held purpose and meaning? You do not always have to be the recipient of an artifact. You can also provide it to others so they share in the significance. Whatever the object, if it holds significance to you; find it, keep it and capture the memory for the future.

Thought: *Artifacts are those key symbolic relics we hold on to because of the purpose and meaning it might hold.*

Question: *Describe something that you hold on to that is symbolic and significant. Tell what it is in detail and why it is so important to you.*

~ Your Reflections ~

_____

_____

_____

_____

_____

_____

_____

_____

_____

_____

_____

_____

_____

_____

_____

_____

_____

_____

_____

_____

_____

_____

_____

~ Easy to be difficult ~

What am I entitled to? What have I earned based on my years of experience and results? Unfortunately, life is not based on a point system like travel rewards that you can cash out for an exotic vacation. You may think that you have accomplished many things and should be provided certain advantages because you have paid your dues. I would even say some individuals feel they deserve things to come easier as a result. Surprisingly, some of those who feel most entitled have not even accomplished much in their young lives. The opposite also holds where some of the most established people I know feel that they still need to work hard to achieve and accomplish things.

I have never felt that I should be given priority or an easy path. Just look at the stack of rejection letters I have received upon graduating from university. People wonder why I always take a more difficult and complicated route. I guess it is because the easy path does not offer the challenge and the self-fulfillment I desire. I also find the easy path is already crowded by many people who are trying to work along it and not really appreciating the journey. The path I travel is far less crowded and allows me the room to be creative and innovative.

My schedule and life is always busy and it is often self-inflicted as I cram a lot of activity into my day. I once sat on a panel for work-life balance and people laughed at my participation because they felt that I worked too hard; putting in long hours and had no concept of balance. My response was that I actually had a better grasp of work-life balance than most others because I had found my calling and am never sure where work starts and pleasure ends. It is all about perspective.

I personally do not want things given to me; I have always felt I needed to earn it. If I did not earn it, then I am not immersed into the journey and not as interested in the result. I select the things that will engage me and realize that I am a dreamer and a doer. Entitlement is not something that interests me because I enjoy taking something that does not exist or is dysfunctional and try to vision, build and implement a solution.

Again, people may say that I make things more difficult or more complicated than they need to be and perhaps I do, but in the end, the result is always worth it. I always like to think of my life in this way, "The more difficult the struggle, the sweeter the prize." It is a sweet deal that I have going on!

Thought: *We sometimes feel like we are entitled to things in life when in fact we should earn them.*

Question: *If you were given an opportunity that provided certainty and an easy path or uncertainty and a challenge, which do you prefer and why?*

~ Your Reflections ~

_____

_____

_____

_____

_____

_____

_____

_____

_____

_____

_____

_____

_____

_____

_____

_____

_____

_____

_____

_____

_____

~ Reflection on self and around ~

There is a valuable life story by Epictetus that I would like to share. What is great about this storyteller is that he wonderfully balances and applies philosophy to ordinary people. His basic principle focuses on *"How do I live a happy, fulfilling life? How can I be a good person?"*

Epcitetus was Marcus Aurelius' teacher and similar to Sun Tzu and the *Art of War*, his writings were considered a military manual. He lived countless centuries ago but his writings still hold true. They centered around three aspects:

1. Mastering your desires;
2. Honourably performing your duties; and
3. Learn about yourself and your relations with the larger community

One of my favorite pieces by Epictetus is where he talked about a young man who would go down to a pond every morning; look in to the depth and leave, only to return the next day. This went on for many years and he grew to be a just, strong and powerful leader. Then one day, he stopped coming.

The ground that the man walked upon talked to the water and asked, *"Did you notice the young man who used to come here every morning does not come here anymore? His presence was light and graceful."* To that, the water replied, *"What man? I do not recall seeing a man. When did he come by?"*

The ground was surprised and said, *"Every day for many years. What do you mean you did not see him?"* The water then suddenly realized the tragedy and replied, *"Oh my, every morning I had the opportunity to see something but did not realize that it was a man because I was so focused on looking into the depth of the pools of water that were looking down at me (the great man's eyes) trying to see my own reflection."*

What I appreciate about this story besides beautifully told, is that while this great man used to come down every morning, but the pond was so focused on itself and its own vanity, that it missed a tremendous opportunity to see greatness. It is a reminder that we must be able to

understand ourselves but not to the extent we forget about what is going on around us.

There is a balance to be had. I think that if you are so focused externally, you forget what you hold. Equally, if you are so focused internally, you are never really aware of what exists around you and how it might help you in your journey. I think the best way is to look in the mirror and in the reflection, also look at you in your surroundings.

Thought: *There are times we focus internally and other times we focus externally. There is a need to understand ourselves better.*

Question: *When you look in the mirror, what do you see? Write about what you see in the mirror when you see your reflection. This can be physically or deeper within you.*

~ Your Reflections ~

~ Time out...take time to think, take time to share ~

Looking forward, time seems infinite. Looking back, it seems far too quick. As our first year students to the university come in, they feel that graduation is at the end of a long road and it is going to be a challenging journey to reach it. Students who recently graduated told me they could not believe how fast their time at SFU came and went. One thing is certain, time is a constant, it does not go faster or slower, we do.

 Looking back at 2012, I turned 50 and where have the years gone? It does not seem that long ago when I was crossing the stage at SFU and started my own professional journey. I have gone from being a janitor, retail manager, claims adjuster, road safety coordinator, community consultation manager, manager of student engagement, community/alumni relations, instructor, blogger and writer. Thirty years of work experience has provided me with rich and valuable experiences that I can share with others. Along the way I have captured my stories and life lessons and they are stacked upon each other and support all aspects of my life. We all have life lessons; sometimes we do not realize their significance till later in life.

Whether you are at the dawn of your career or, like me on the cusp of the sunset, what are you grasping and learning? What are you gathering so you can share with others in the future?

At the beginning of your career, you may have felt like you did not have much to share. I would say that you do. You have transitioned from student to professional and that experience would benefit those who are only a few years behind you. Never feel that you might not have the experience, you do. What you can share now will likely be different than what you can share in ten years' time. Twenty years further will be different again. You will always have something to share. Sometimes your experiences will be new and sometimes they will supplement what you already know. For now, take the time to understand what you gather. Time does not stand still.

Thought: *We all have something to share based on our accumulated experience and knowledge.*

Question: *If you had an opportunity to share your insight with someone else, what would you say and who would you say it to?*

~ Your Reflections ~

_____

_____

_____

_____

_____

_____

_____

_____

_____

_____

_____

_____

_____

_____

_____

_____

_____

_____

_____

_____

_____

_____

_____

~ Being a bucket or a candle ~

I often get asked how I can keep pace with being optimistic on a constant basis day in and day out. How can someone look at the positive side of life even amidst adversity? Don't things get you down? Don't negative people pull you down?

Sure, if you hold a life where you see the glass half full, it can be a challenge at times but you have to ask yourself if you are a bucket or a candle. What I mean by this is that if you see yourself as a large bucket filled with optimism and those around you as smaller empty buckets around and you pour your contents into their container as you come in contact with them. In this situation, what is happening? As they are taking from you, you are getting depleted. This is not sustainable for anyone who might be that big bucket.

Instead, if you change your perspective to one where you see yourself as a lit candle and those around you as a room of unlit candles. As you engage and interact with them, your light will light their candle and there is a bigger flame and as they pull away, you both have an intense flame; however, your  flame is no less depleted and still the same size. Before you know it, the room is lit fully and it is a warm bright glowing space. You are still the same and you can appreciate the radiance around you. If you take time to sit and stare at a candle, you will be amazed at the intensity that the flame holds. It is bright, constant and ever present.

Sometimes you need to focus on your own perspective and determine what makes up who you are. By simply choosing to be a lit candle and not a bucket, you have an easy descriptor to what makes up who you are and the ability to have a perspective on your life. By framing my life as a lit candle, it is what I strive to keep going. I then choose to not let people deplete me. I consider how I can enrich and enable those around me.

A lesson for me is if you see the glass half full or half empty...as community volunteer with a bright candle, I take the light from my candle and go in search with the glass and look for someone thirsty.

Thought: *There are times in our life where we let the environment overwhelm us so we feel like a bucket or internally we control the situation and feel like a candle.*

Question: *Do you feel you are more of a bucket or a candle? Think of a situation where you were a bucket or a candle and write about the experience.*

~ Your Reflections ~

_____

_____

_____

_____

_____

_____

_____

_____

_____

_____

_____

_____

_____

_____

_____

_____

_____

_____

_____

_____

_____

_____

~ Do you want to watch or be in the parade? ~

Growing up I had the opportunity to see many parades and eventually, I was not satisfied by just seeing the parade; one day, I wanted to be in the parade! You dream it and then do it! What is your parade?

In my case, a good friend of mine was the Pipe Major of a small military pipe band and said they were looking for drummers. Keep in mind; I am not a musically inclined person. He provided me with an opportunity to try out for the part and instead of shying away, I faced it head on. I went to his house on a Tuesday and had a practice session with the other five members. The Pipe Major asked me, *"Sam, I realize you have never drummed or paraded or marched. The drumming you can learn but what I need is commitment. Can you commit to be a part of the band and show up for practices and performances?"* I replied with a resounding yes because I knew I would be able to commit myself. Friday the same week, I went to the regimental drill hall to get my uniform and drum and to watch the band. There I stood, uniform and drum in hand and my Pipe Major said, *"Okay everyone fall in, we are about to parade and perform for the regiment. Sam, that includes you."* With a smile, the Pipe Major told me that all I need to do is hit the drum for every step we take and follow the person in front of me (and be thankful you are not the one leading). With that, I started my 11 year term with the BC Regiment Irish Pipes and Drums.

I marched in many parades, performed at many events, and became the communications officer. I helped publicize our band, attained the rank of Corporal and helped grow our band to 25 members. I realized my dream of being in a parade. What have you wanted to do but sat on the side lines to watch instead? Could it be stepping on the ice and learning to skate, learning a new language so you could travel to a different place? The key is that you can learn any of these things but the key ingredient is commitment. Commitment will drive you to accomplish what you set out to do. It goes back to whether you are a dreamer or a doer. Make a commitment to do something and then stick to this one thing till it is done. This has helped me to accomplish the many things in my life. I was never the best drummer in the band, but I still made a valuable contribution, I thoroughly enjoyed the experience. Vision it, commit to it and then do it and don't forget to have fun along the way!

Thought: *There are times that we sit and watch a parade or that we can get up and be in the parade.*

Question: *What is it that you are doing right now that has you sitting on the sidelines? What would you like to do about it so you can start doing instead of watching?*

~ Your Reflections ~

_____

_____

_____

_____

_____

_____

_____

_____

_____

_____

_____

_____

_____

_____

_____

_____

_____

_____

_____

_____

_____

_____

_____

_____

~ Laying a foundation to completion ~

How does one go from a singular thought to a full blown book that is about to launch? Three years ago, I would never have thought...so what happened? It was about -

- being a dreamer and a doer – if you dream of doing it then put it to action
- not being afraid to reach out to the people around you to ask for support and help
- believing in your ideas – no matter how crazy and far-fetched it might be
- being patient and letting your thoughts glide along
- not letting those voices around you tell you that you can't/shouldn't do it
- holding realistic expectations on what you can accomplish
- taking things in bite sized format and not dwelling on the magnitude of how big it really is
- not holding on to a structured format that does not allow one to make changes
- understanding it is a journey – you are in this for the long haul
- writing for yourself and knowing that an audience is out there who will appreciate what you say
- being true to you

This is what I can realistically say has been my foundation for this book. Scattered stories in my mind and in documents that sat idle, came together once I realized these thoughts. This has certainly been a journey. There were times where it became a struggle but my thought was always about finishing this book and not letting it slip out of my hands. I owned this and it was for me. Something for me to share with others.

It is now at the finishing stages and collecting my thoughts above, it transfers to anything you want to accomplish in life. Adhere to the points that matter to you. The ones listed above are mine and some may relate to you; however, what helps you? If you look at my list, there is overlap to many things we try to accomplish in life. Look around you. What have you started that sits idle? What would you like to start but you are not sure where to begin?

As I near a finish line for the book, there is a new milestone – the book launch. A celebration of the journey and building something that will carry the book forward. The book launch is for me…but it is also for those who have been on the journey with me.

For me, the puzzle analogy has been a constant and the book is similar to a box with puzzle pieces. Slowly, I had to take the pieces and see how they fit. Some times you hold a piece and put it aside because you are not sure how it connects. There were times where I had to walk away so I could clear my thoughts. In my mind, there was no question that I was going to finish this puzzle…and while there are still a few scattered pieces, I have a good idea what it is looking like.

Thought: We all have things that need to be done and strive to complete it and at times it can be difficult without a process or thoughts

Question: What would you like to accomplish and have you outlined how you will do this? What are the important aspects for you to consider?

~ Your Reflections ~

_____

_____

_____

_____

_____

_____

_____

_____

_____

_____

_____

_____

_____

Concluding Remarks

"If you don't know the trees you may be lost in the forest, but if you don't know the stories you may be lost in life."
~ *Siberian Elder* ~

This book may have focused on storytelling, but it was also about you. If you purchased this book because you wanted to know more about personal storytelling, then you have started your journey. If you were already reflective, I hope that you were able to find some comfort in the stories I have shared and some new perspectives to think about.

We all have something to say and we all have something to share but unfortunately we do not always think it is worth telling. Believe me, there is an audience out there waiting for you to share your journey.

The beginning of this book started with the words: "What's the last story you heard? What's the last story you told? What's the last story you've lived?" These words are the essence of this book. We hear stories, we tell stories, but have we incorporated the stories into our life? The book hopefully prompted you, through storytelling, to focus on your own life and lessons that you might bring to make some sense and purpose of the things that happen around you.

The intent was to provide a path to help unlock your personal storytelling. Part One provided background on what is storytelling and foundation on what makes up stories while Part Two focused on CARPE Diem as a method to help capture your stories. Part Three provided some additional tools to form your stories while Part Four used excerpts from my blog to provide you with the opportunity to reflect and try your hand at writing.

Completing this book does not make you an instant story writer/teller as that takes more time. My intent was to share the process that has helped me become a better storyteller. I have shared my experiences to help you unlock the skills to storytelling while becoming self-reflective and looking within yourself for different stories and opportunities. I have shared some of my life lessons to help you pull meaningful insight.

Much like the puzzle analogy provided at the outset of Part Three, your stories become pieces of a larger jigsaw puzzle. Situations and incidents may not make sense in the immediate but what is required is that you catalogue them for the future. These pieces start to make sense and you begin to see how it all comes together. The more you sharpen your senses, the more that the pieces become representative of you and reminder pieces to make sense of your life puzzle.

So what are your next steps? Where do you want to take storytelling? Do you want to journal and learn more about you or do you want to start sharing your journey? Or, perhaps you want to both? It really is all about you and where you decided to go with your personal stories. If you feel you have a new perspective or way to look at things, please let me know. If you found that this unlocked some hidden potential within you, then please share it with me. If you now feel like writing (three years ago I never imagined myself as a writer) then please start.

This has certainly been a journey for me. I never thought that writing was a skillset I had until it was exposed via my blog and it grew in importance to me. I also made a commitment and stuck to it. This was a marathon of sorts but through the community of champions and enablers, I was able to conclude this adventure.

Be open to what life provides you and understand it is not always obvious. Stories will be swimming all around you. Capture small nuggets and hold on to them and try to find the purpose and meaning around the experiences you encounter. If I can find the extraordinary in the ordinary, what are you missing?

I have spoken about the puzzle analogy and have woven it throughout this book. It is an important understanding on the journey to build your life puzzle and the connectedness we share. I want to take this opportunity to offer you a puzzle piece from me so that we are connected and that you are also connected to a community of storytellers and change makers. By supporting my journey here, you have earned a piece and connection to me. For that I am grateful and appreciative. Please drop me a note at story.share.community@gmail.com and request a puzzle piece. You can also use this email or my http://sam-thiara.com to share your stories with me or your thoughts about storytelling or check on what I am up to at @Sam_Thiara on Twitter. In the spirit of this book, partial proceeds from sales will go towards community initiatives and projects on a regional, national and international level to help change lives one person at a time.

Go forward and build an amazing autobiography. In my eyes, there is nothing ordinary about you, you are only extraordinary. You have the capacity to do spectacular things in life, but make sure to capture and share them. I do sincerely thank you for taking the time to read my words as it has been a labour of love.

"The ending is a new beginning. More adventures, more stories and more people to meet. Once I print this book, I will think to myself…Oh I should have shared this or told them that. Let's save it for the next time we meet."
~Sam Thiara~

~NOTES & THOUGHTS~

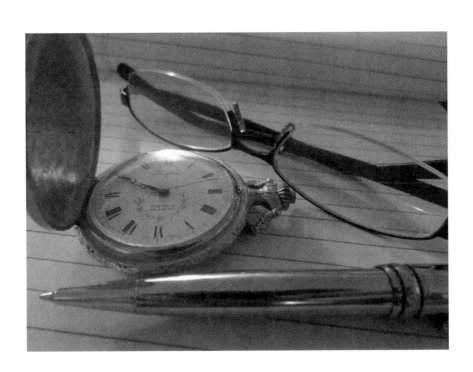

~ Notes ~

~ Notes ~

~ Notes ~

~ Notes ~

~ Notes ~

~ Notes ~

~ Notes ~

~ Notes ~

~ Notes ~

~ Notes ~

~ Notes ~

~ Notes ~

~ Notes ~

~ Notes ~

~ Notes ~

~ Notes ~

~ Notes ~

~ Notes ~

Sources:

1) "Curiosity." Dictionary.com. Dictionary.com, n.d. Web. 26 Mar. 2014.
http://dictionary.reference.com/browse/curiosity?s=t
2) "Appreciation." Dictionary.com. Dictionary.com, n.d. Web. 26 Mar. 2014.
http://dictionary.reference.com/browse/appreciation?s=t
3) "Reflection." Dictionary.com. Dictionary.com, n.d. Web. 26 Mar. 2014.
http://dictionary.reference.com/browse/reflection?s=t
4) "Perspective." Dictionary.com. Dictionary.com, n.d. Web. 26 Mar. 2014.
http://dictionary.reference.com/browse/perspective?s=t
5) "Experience." Dictionary.com. Dictionary.com, n.d. Web. 26 Mar. 2014.
http://dictionary.reference.com/browse/experience?s=t

~ ABOUT THE AUTHORS ~

Sam and Adam – the joint work

Sam and Adam first met at Simon Fraser University, where Sam was working in student engagement and Adam was an engaged student. Being naturally relationship-oriented, they established a fast friendship and upon Adam's graduation and joining SFU's business school as staff, the two furthered their connection as colleagues. It seemed they were brought together by their shared appreciation for people, leadership and education.

In 2011 Sam and Adam were chatting over a tea and Sam mentioned his vision for this book. There were ideas and thoughts that made the foundation, but Sam wondered where to go with it. By speaking to Adam, Sam realized that both of them could be a part of this adventure – and so an opportunity for collaboration was born.

Over the many months that followed, the structure was built and substance was added. Adam was instrumental at the outset to help the vision take shape and added much to the ideas and content as a contributing author. A person could approach the endeavour of writing on one's own, however, having someone to talk with and contribute to the writing helped to create this book.

MEET THE AUTHORS - Sam (Ajit)Thiara

 Through his tireless work, Sam continues to be committed to the betterment of communities. In 2012 he received the Queen's Diamond Jubilee Medal and in 2006, he received the Governor General's Caring Canadian Award for leadership and community involvement. His passion is to inspire and motivate others in their personal and professional development through his many adventures and reflections on life's journey.

As a compelling storyteller and accomplished speaker, audiences appreciate the sincerity and authenticity that Sam brings forward. Whether it is as a keynote speaker to hundreds or mentoring a single person, Sam finds time to be a part of your journey. He has helped thousands and mentored hundreds in their pursuit of their dreams.

Sam is currently pursuing his dream of publishing this book, teaching and launching a mentorship/coaching venture. Most recently, Sam worked at the Beedie School of Business at Simon Fraser University as Associate Director, Undergraduate Community Relations. He also has a background at SFU in student engagement, alumni relations and community outreach. Prior to this, he has worked with organizations like the Vancouver 2010 Olympic Bid Committee and ICBC's road safety department. Sam has dedicated countless hours to over 30+ not-for-profit organizations at the board, advisory and volunteer levels.

Sam received his MA in Leadership Studies at the University of Exeter in England and has a double major in Business Administration and Political Science from SFU. He also completed a number of personal development programs in teaching, leadership and human resources.

Sam consistently strives to discover the extraordinary in the ordinary and his journey is documented at www.sam-thiara.com

"Everyone's life is an autobiography...make yours worth reading!"

Adam Cotterall - Contributing Author

 Adam has dedicated his career to teaching, coaching and human capital consulting, as means by which to live his mission of "growing himself to better help others grow". He is privileged to have played a part in the evolving careers of thousands of students and clients.

As an Executive Search Consultant with North America's premier executive recruitment firm, Caldwell Partners International, Adam helps companies find and attract leadership talent that will write the next chapter of the company's story. Adam also teaches courses in Leadership, Organizational Effectiveness, Performance Management, and Organizational Behaviour at SFU's Beedie School of Business.

Adam held prior positions as Vice President of Client Services at Right Management, the world's largest talent and career management consulting firm, and Associate Director of the Learning Strategies Group and Executive Education at SFU's Segal Graduate School of Business.

With a passion and fascination for learning about leadership and organizational effectiveness, Adam holds an MBA from Queen's University, a BBA with a Joint Major in Psychology from SFU, and is a Certified Human Resources Professional.

Serving as the 2011 Chair of the BC Human Resources Management Association Annual Conference, Adam is also an active member of the Vancouver Board of Trade and Business Council of BC, receiving several awards recognizing his community contributions as a speaker, facilitator and committee member. On weekends, Adam can often be found playing the role of photographer's assistant to his remarkable wife, Lyndsay.

Ignite the Dream Consulting

I hope that by inspiring your story voice, you will take the time to share your stories with me. Tell me about something that is meaningful to you. I look forward to collecting a community of stories. If something is important to you, it is worth building a story around it.

To find out what I am up to, reach out and share your stories with me and to keep in touch, please see or contact me at:

Email: story.share.community@gmail.com

Website: http://sam-thiara.com

Twitter: @Sam_Thiara

TEDxSFU Talk: http://tedxtalks.ted.com/video/TEDxSFU-Sam-Thiara

Linked In: http://www.linkedin.com/pub/sam-thiara/0/889/911